CROBOTS

20 amigurumi robots to make

CROBOTS

20 amigurumi robots to make

NELLY PAILLOUX

Andrews McMeel Publishing, LLC

Kansas City

Crobots

ANDREWS McMEEL PUBLISHING, LLC
An Andrews McMeel Universal company
1130 Walnut Street
Kansas City, Missouri 64106

ISBN-13: 978-0-7407-7827-8
ISBN-10: 0-7407-7827-7

This book was conceived, designed, and produced by
Ivy Press
210 High Street
Lewes
East Sussex BN7 2NS, U.K.
www.ivy-group.co.uk

Creative Director Peter Bridgewater
Publisher Jason Hook
Editorial Director Tom Kitch
Senior Editor Lorraine Turner
Art Director Wayne Blades
Concept Design Linda Becker
Design Clare Barber
Illustrations Melvyn Evans
Photographer Andrew Perris

Originated and printed in China

12 11 10 9 8 7 6 5 4 3 2 1

Important!
Safety warning: Crobots are not toys. Many have small, removable parts and should be kept out of the reach of small children.

CONTENTS

INTRODUCTION

Isn't there something contradictory about the idea of a crochet robot? Aren't robots tough and unyielding? Not necessarily! Meet the crobots. The 20 little creatures in this book are all cute, soft, and useful. Each one can be given a job to do, whether it's keeping an eye on your desk (step forward, Geisha) or guarding your keys (meet the alert and sparky Dogbot), although you have to be careful that covetous people don't carry them off while they're hard at work.

Best of all, you can make any or all of the crobots yourself. This collection represents the sweetest, tiniest trend in amigurumi since . . . well, since amigurumi was invented. Neatly crocheted in a host of colors ranging from the subtle to the brilliant, crobots demonstrate that even the smallest woolen creatures can have distinct personalities. Crobots make great confidantes (they're small enough to put in a pocket or a purse, and tough enough to survive daily one-on-one sharing sessions). They make good gifts, too, and you can personalize them according to the needs and interests of each recipient, tweaking the color mix, adding a sequin or two, or even mixing and matching characteristics between crobots to create entirely new characters.

If you're a keen crochet maven, you'll find that you can make even the most feature-laden crobot in a couple of evenings. If you've never picked up a crochet hook before, there are easy-to-follow instructions to guide you. We've arranged the patterns in order of difficulty, so if you don't have much crochet experience or are not used to working on a small scale, start with one of the patterns at the beginning of the book and work up to the (slightly) more challenging ones near the end. Picking one of the easier patterns will ensure that you finish it—successfully—while you're still practicing your crochet-hook skills.

Despite their tiny size, crobots are not toys. Make sure you keep them well out of reach of small children.

CROCHETING THE CROBOTS

Read these pages before you start!

Making the crobots isn't hard if you have basic crocheting skills. Even if you don't, it's quite easy to learn, and the basic steps are shown on these pages. Most of the crobots are worked in spirals, like all little amigurumi dolls. You do not have to join rounds, but if you want a foolproof way to count rows, use a stitch marker or a paper clip to mark the end of each round and move it up as you complete each round. The squared-off parts of the crobots are worked in rows—that is, you chain one, then turn at the end of each row.

WHAT YOU NEED

Each crobot has an ingredients list at the start of the pattern, which includes everything you need. The yarn used for the crobots is always light worsted weight (10 ply, or #3).

The patterns for the crobots do not give yarn quantities because the quantities for even the largest bot are very small and the amount needed will vary according to how loosely or tightly you crochet. For the main color of each crobot, you are likely to use no more than about half a 1.75 oz (50 g) ball of double-knit yarn. We suggest that you buy complete balls of yarn for your first couple of crobots and then, when you have a good idea of how much yarn they require, move on to some of your remnants from other knitting or crocheting projects.

All the crobot patterns use a C2 (2.75 mm) crochet hook. If you're an experienced amigurumi maker, you may want to choose an even smaller hook (the smaller the hook, the daintier your crobots will be), but if you're less experienced, a very fine hook may be too fiddly at first.

STARTING WITH CROBOTS

Each crobot is made in separate pieces—heads, arms, legs, and so on. They are usually joined together once the crocheting is complete, but sometimes you'll receive an instruction to stuff a body or head and close up the gap as you go along. Be sure to follow these instructions—they will make your crobot easier to put together in the end.

SKILL LEVEL

The crobots are marked with one to four cogwheels to indicate how easy they are to make. Start with a single-cogwheel crobot and work up to the slightly more complex ones.

How to make a foundation chain

This is the starting point of all crochet patterns.

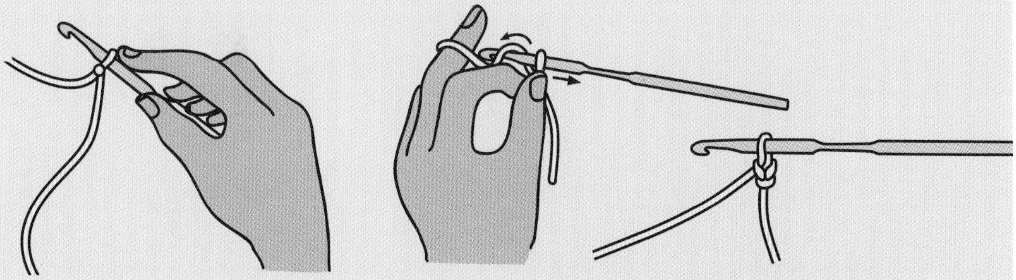

1 Make a slip knot by making a loop, then hooking the length of yarn through it with your hook and pulling to tighten.

2 Start a foundation chain by bringing the yarn over the hook from the back to the front, and grabbing it with the hook. Draw the yarn through the knot and onto the hook to make your first chain stitch. Repeat to add stitches to the chain.

How to increase

To increase, you need to work two stitches into the first stitch of a row. Work the first stitch as usual, then use your hook to pull an extra stitch through the loop beneath.

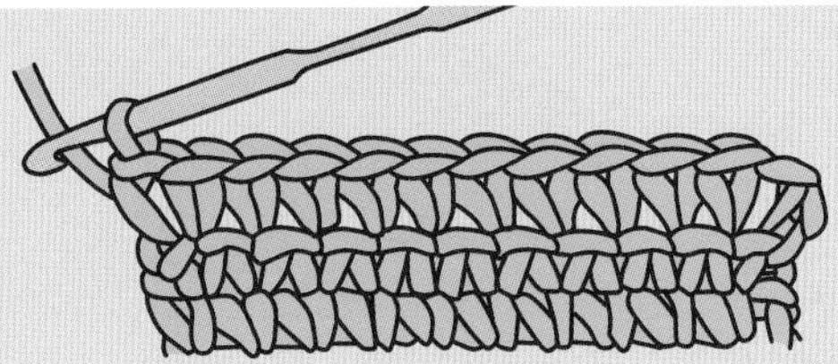

How to decrease

Draw up two loops onto your hook (adding to the stitch already on the hook) by feeding the hook through the next two stitches in line. With three loops on the hook, place your yarn over the hook and draw it through all three loops to decrease one stitch.

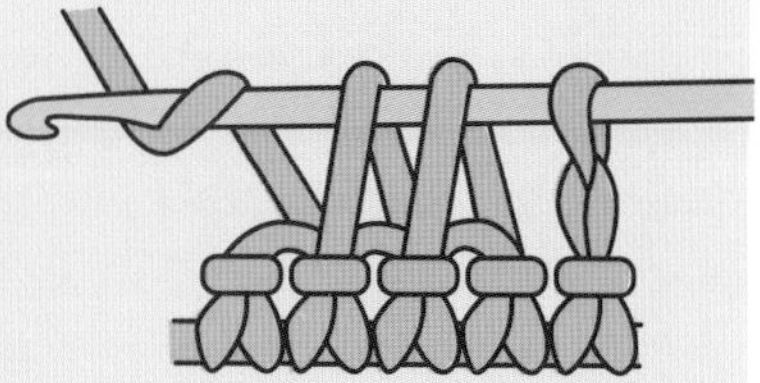

BASIC CROCHET STITCHES

Crobots use only three crochet stitches: slip stitch, single, and half-double.

Slip stitch (sl)

Slip stitch is the most basic crochet stitch of all. It is particularly useful for finishing off edges or joining pieces together.

1 Start with a foundation chain. Insert the hook into the second chain from the hook, then pass it under and hook the yarn.

2 Draw through the chain and loop already on the hook to make one slip stitch.

3 Continue working into the next stitch in the row.

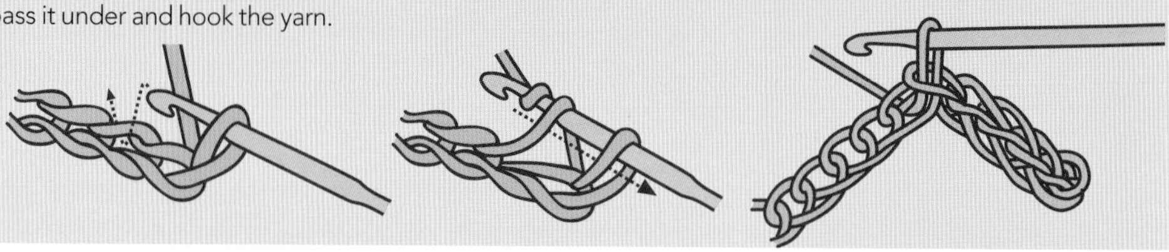

Single crochet (sc)

Insert the hook into the next chain, pass it under and hook the yarn. Draw the loop through the first chain on the hook. Then hook under the yarn again, and draw this through the two loops.

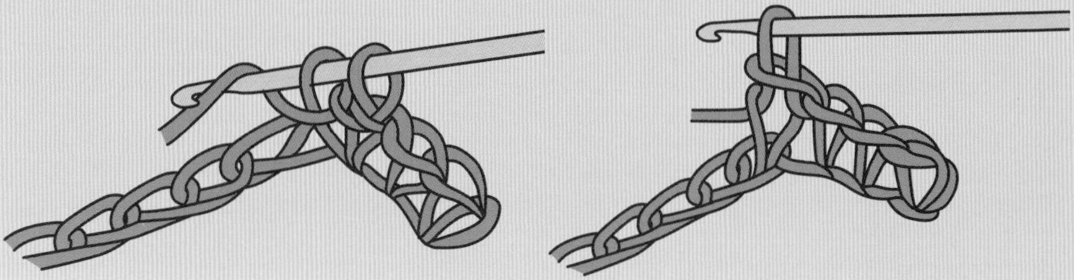

Half-double crochet (hdc)

Put the yarn over the hook. Insert the hook into the third stitch to be worked, then place the yarn over the hook again and pull it through the loop. Place the yarn over the hook again, then pull it through all three loops on the hook. This makes one half-double crochet stitch.

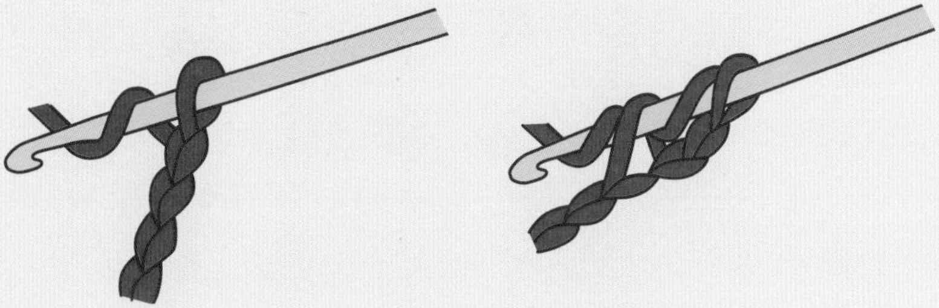

Making a magic ring

Amigurumi dolls are almost always made this way: It's a method of crocheting a neat, tight, circle without leaving a central hole.

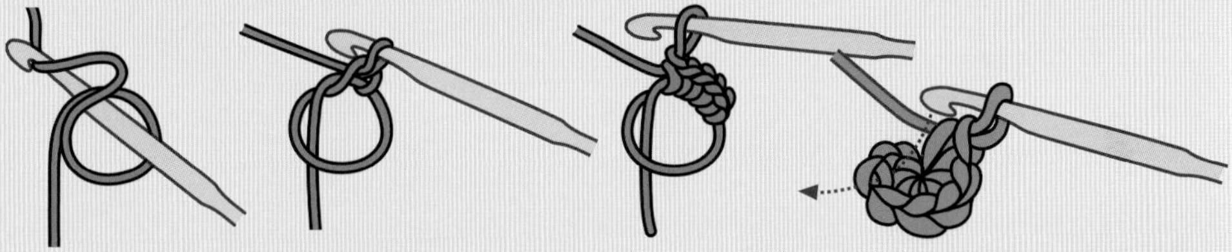

1 Make a large circle with your yarn, leaving a trailing tail, then use the hook to draw the working yarn through both the circle and tail strand held together. This creates one loop.

2 With this loop, chain one stitch to begin the magic ring.

3 Continue making single chain stitches around the ring, following the number of stitches required for the pattern until you have worked a full circle. Pull the tail of yarn to close the ring and make a tight round.

4 Begin your second round by crocheting into the first stitch of the first round, Use a paper clip or a stitch marker to mark the beginning of the new round.

MAKING UP THE CROBOTS

Putting a crobot together isn't difficult, but it can be detailed. Make some of the simpler models first—the book starts with the easiest and ends with more challenging models. A neat finish adds a lot to the charm of these little bots, so it's worth a little extra effort to give them as much polish as possible.

Stuffing amigurumi

Use a customized toy stuffing. These are light, soft, and easy to use—don't be tempted to go for cotton balls or any other options, as they may give lumpy or hard results. A properly built crobot feels firm but soft when you squeeze it. Pack the stuffing in bit by bit. Sometimes the gap is quite small, or you need to sew most of it up before stuffing the crobot; in this case, you may find it helpful to use a matchstick or a toothpick to pack wisps of stuffing into the corners.

Sewing together

You can use either yarn, sewing thread, or a single thread of embroidery floss to sew your crobots together. If you choose to use the tail of yarn, use a yarn needle. Otherwise, use sewing thread or a single strand of embroidery floss in a color to match the bot. Sew the pieces together in the order suggested, knot the ends of the thread, and stitch the end through the crobot, cutting it off close to the surface.

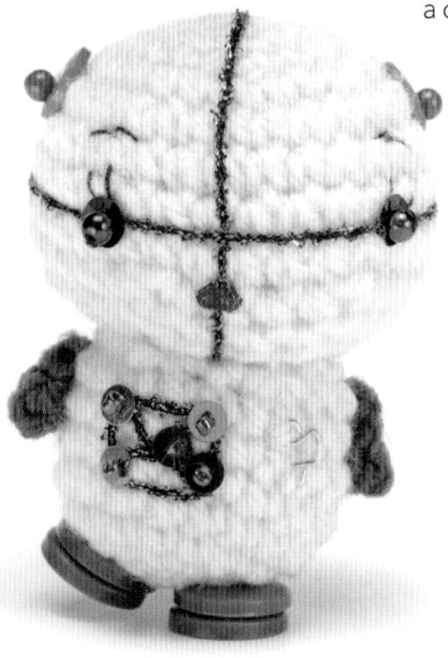

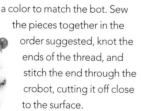

Embroidery stitches

Standard embroidery floss comes in a small skein. The thread is made up of six separate strands, which you can pull apart to get the thickness you want (in most of the crobot instructions, floss will be used in single or double threads, although if you're embroidering French knots, use three strands). Cut a short length of floss (12 to 16 inches long) and simply separate the strands at one end, then separate the desired number of strands from the main piece. Use the size of embroidery needle you feel most comfortable with—it's easier to work on a small scale with a relatively small needle, but the tiniest embroidery needles can be hard to handle unless you're used to fine sewing. If you plan to add beads as well as stitches, use a beading needle—this is a narrow needle with an equally narrow head, made to pass through the holes of even the tiniest beads.

If you are embroidering facial features on a crobot and want to make sure you get the positioning just right, you may find an erasable pen useful. These can be purchased at craft stores and are used for marking on fabric—the lines will disappear completely after a few days.

You can either tie a small knot at the end of the floss or make a tiny cross stitch (one stitch laid over another) to anchor it before beginning to embroider. Finish off in the same way. It's worth practicing your stitches—French knots, in particular, can take a few tries to get right.

Some of the embroidery is done on pieces of felt and then attached to the crobot, while some is sewn directly onto the crocheted yarn. Embroidering directly onto crochet is a little harder—you need to practice making neat, visible stitches, and starting and finishing your work while disguising any tiny finishing-off knots among the crochet stitches.

To overstitch

Overstitching is usually used to attach one piece of fabric to another—for example, a felt control panel to the crocheted body of a crobot. To overstitch, take a single strand of floss or thread, put the panel of fabric to be attached in place, then bring the thread up through both thicknesses (yarn and fabric) and make a small stitch at right angles to the edge of the panel. Push the needle through the yarn, then bring it up again through both crobot body and felt panel, and repeat the stitch. This is a practical rather than a decorative stitch, so use matching thread and make it as neat and unobtrusive as possible.

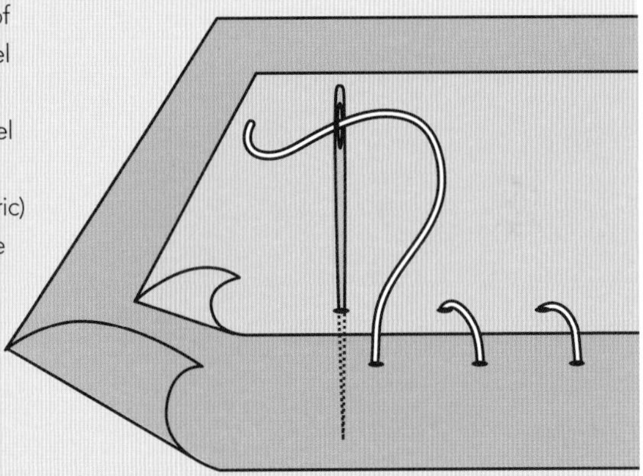

To backstitch

This stitch makes a plain, solid line.

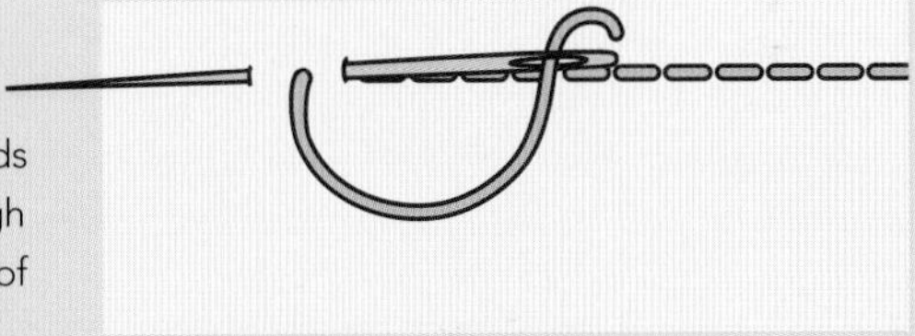

1 Thread a needle with either one or two strands of thread, as directed, then bring it up through the fabric at the point at which you want the line of stitching to start.

2 Make a stitch going the opposite way from the way you want your backstitch line to continue, and bring the needle back up through the fabric one stitch's length away in the direction in which you want your stitching to go.

3 Take the thread backward and push the needle through the point where the first stitch finished. Bring it out again the same distance (one stitch's length) in front of the thread. Continue in the same way until the length of the desired line of backstitch is complete.

To chain stitch

This stitch makes a decorative row of linked loops, rather like a row of crochet pressed flat.

1 Bring your needle up through the fabric, then bring the spare thread out in front of your needle and make a loop around it. Reinsert the needle in the fabric and bring it out again one stitch's length in front of your first stitch, and through the loop of thread.

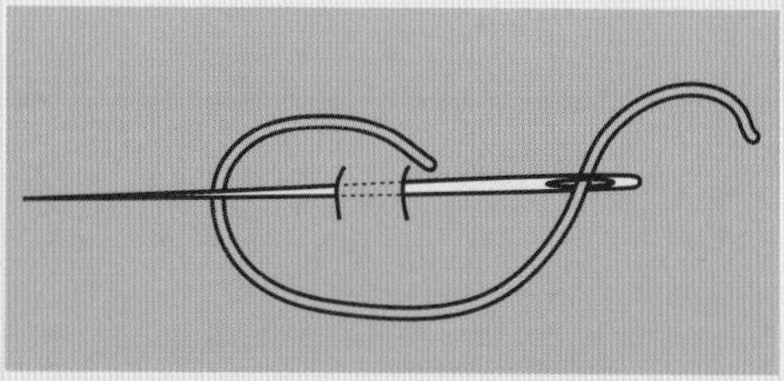

2 Pull the thread tight to make an oval-shaped stitch. Repeat both steps to make a chain of looped stitches.

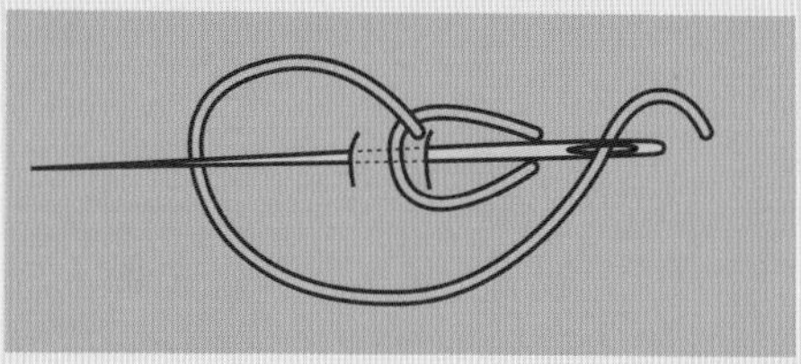

To satin stitch

This stitch is useful for filling small areas.

To cover small areas with colored stitching, the easiest way is to make single, long, parallel stitches (usually with two strands of thread) close together. This will make a solid area of threads.

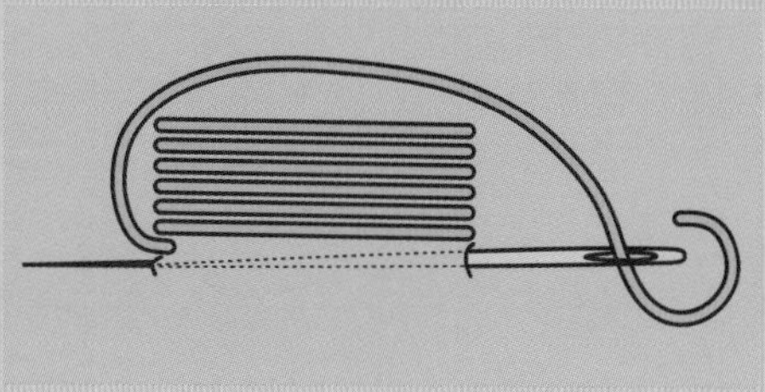

To make a French knot

This stitch makes a small, decorative knot that stands above the surface of the yarn or fabric.

1 Thread the needle with three strands of floss, fasten the end, and bring it out at the point at which you want to make your French knot. With your left thumb, hold the thread down at the point where it emerges from the fabric and wrap it twice around the needle.

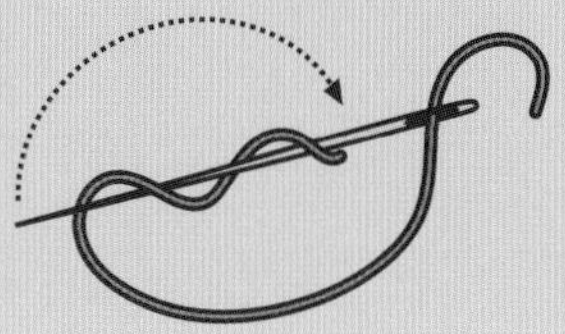

2 Keeping your thumb in place on the fabric, bring the needle back to the starting point and put the point back through the fabric very near where it emerged (not in the exact same spot, though—or the thread will simply pull back through the hole).

3 Pull the needle to the back of the fabric and pull taut. This will leave a small, textured knot. Tie off the thread at the back or go on to make the next French knot.

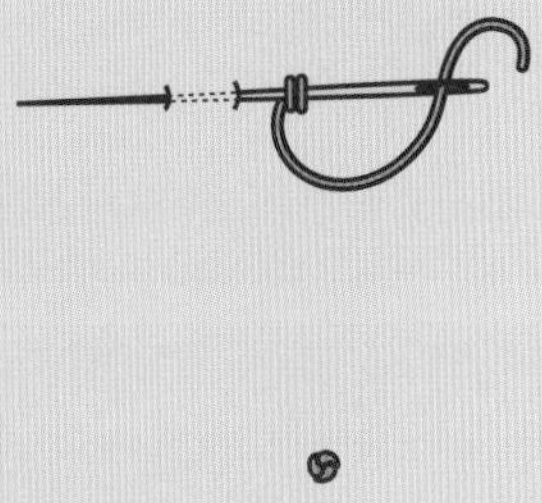

Beading

Always use a beading needle to add beads and sequins—if you forget and use an embroidery needle, there will be a moment of intense frustration when you find that the needle won't fit through the tiniest bead!

Beads are sewn on simply by bringing the needle through from the back of the fabric, threading the bead onto the needle, and then pushing the needle back through near the original place it emerged and pulling the thread tight.

To add a sequin, you can either bring the needle up through the fabric, threading the sequin on, and then securing it by taking a stitch over to the edge on each side (or more stitches, to make a decorative star shape on top of your sequin), or use a bead to secure it in the center, as shown below.

To secure a sequin with a bead

1 Thread a beading needle and bring it up through the fabric. Thread first a sequin, then a bead, onto the needle.

2 Take the thread back through the central hole of the sequin with the beading needle, pull it tight, and secure at the back of the fabric. The bead, larger than the central hole of the sequin, will hold it in place.

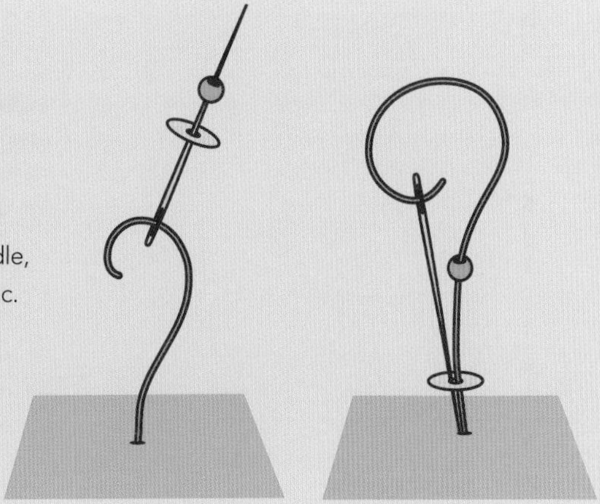

DOGBOT

Just like people, crobots have pets, too. You might mistake Dogbot for a regular doggy companion at first glance, but look closer and you'll notice a row of tiny green switches on his side. And although his expression is friendly, his eyes are set wider and more vertically than most common breeds. His upright tail and lively demeanor, though, are characteristically canine.

YOU WILL NEED

- crochet hook, size C2 (2.75 mm)
- stitch marker or paper clip
- 1 yarn needle
- 1 embroidery needle
- toy stuffing to stuff the bot
- beige yarn
- black yarn (a tiny quantity, for the paws)
- black embroidery floss (2 strands)
- beige embroidery floss (1 strand)
- white embroidery floss (1 strand)
- 3 green beads, ⅛ inch (4 mm) in diameter
- 2 black bugle beads, ¼ inch (7 mm) long
- scrap of white felt, for the face visor

SKILL LEVEL

TO MAKE DOGBOT

To make the head, using beige yarn

Round 1 Start 6 sc in a magic ring (6)
Round 2 2 sc in each sc around (12)
Round 3 *2 sc in next sc, sc in next sc* repeat 6 times (18)
Round 4 *2 sc in next sc, sc in next 2 sc* repeat 6 times (24)
Round 5 *2 sc in next sc, sc in next 3 sc* repeat 6 times (30)
Rounds 6 to 10 1 sc in each sc around (30)
Round 11 *sc dec, sc in next 3 sc* repeat 6 times (24)
Round 12 *sc dec, sc in next 2 sc* repeat 6 times (18)
Stuff firmly
sl st in next sc and tie off, leave long tail to sew to body

To make the ears, using beige yarn

Round 1 Start 4 sc in a magic ring (4)
Round 2 *2 sc in next sc, sc in next sc* repeat twice (6)
Round 3 2 sc in each sc around (12)
Round 4 sc in each sc around (12)
Round 5 *sc dec, sc in next 4 sc* repeat twice (10)
Round 6 sc in each sc around (10)
sl st in next sc and tie off, leave long tail to sew to head. Make 2
No need to stuff

To make the legs, using beige yarn

Round 1 Start 6 sc in a magic ring (6)
Round 2 *2 sc in next sc, sc in next 2 sc* repeat twice (8)
Round 3 in blo for this round sc in each sc around (8)

ABBREVIATIONS: **ch** = *chain* **st** = *stitch* **sl st** = *slip stitch* **sc** = *single crochet* **hdc** = *half-double crochet* **sc dec** = *single crochet decrease (decrease over 2 stitches)* **blo** = *back loops only* ***** = *repeat instructions between asterisks*

Round 4 sc in each sc around (8)
sl st in next sc and tie off, leave long tail to sew to body
Stuff firmly
Make 4

To make the paws, using black yarn
Round 1 Start 6 sc in a magic ring (6)
Round 2 2 sc in each sc around (12)
sl st in next sc and tie off, weave in the end yarn
Make 4

To make the tail, using beige yarn
Round 1 Start 4 sc in a magic ring (4)
Round 2 *2 sc in next sc, sc in next sc* repeat twice (6)
Round 3 sc in each sc around (6)
Round 4 *sc dec, sc in next sc* repeat twice (4)
sl st in next sc and tie off, leave long tail to sew to body
No need to stuff

To make the body, using beige yarn
Round 1 Start 6 sc in a magic ring (6)
Round 2 2 sc in each sc around (12)
Round 3 *2 sc in next sc, sc in next sc* repeat 6 times (18)
Rounds 4 to 12 sc in each sc around (18)
Round 13 *sc dec, sc in next sc* repeat 6 times (12)
Stuff firmly
Round 14 sc dec around (6)
sl st in next sc and tie off, leave long tail to close up the hole

TO ASSEMBLE DOGBOT

- Stuff the head firmly. Flatten the ears, pin them into place, and sew them onto the head using leftover tails of yarn.
- Cut a small rectangle of white felt for the face visor. Sew bead eyes onto each end of the panel, placing them carefully and using one strand of black floss. If you prefer, you may embroider the eyes instead, using long vertical stitches in black floss.
- Sew the visor onto the head, making small overstitches with one strand of white floss.
- Embroider the nose, using two strands of black floss to make a triangular shape with straight horizontal stitches.
- Stuff and close the body, then use one strand of beige yarn to sew on the three bead "switches."
- Stuff each leg. Using one strand of black floss, sew the paws onto the ends of the legs. Attach Dogbot's legs to his body using leftover tails of yarn. Pin Dogbot's tail into place and sew it on.
- Finally, pin Dogbot's head to his body and attach it, using the yarn end to stitch it on.

BLUEPRINT

Dogbot's nose is made from 4 or 5 straight, horizontal stitches, overlapping slightly and getting narrow at the base to give it its triangular shape.

Sew Dogbot's tail on very upright—it gives him a jaunty, confident air.

Attach the face visor with a single strand of white thread, using tiny overstitches.

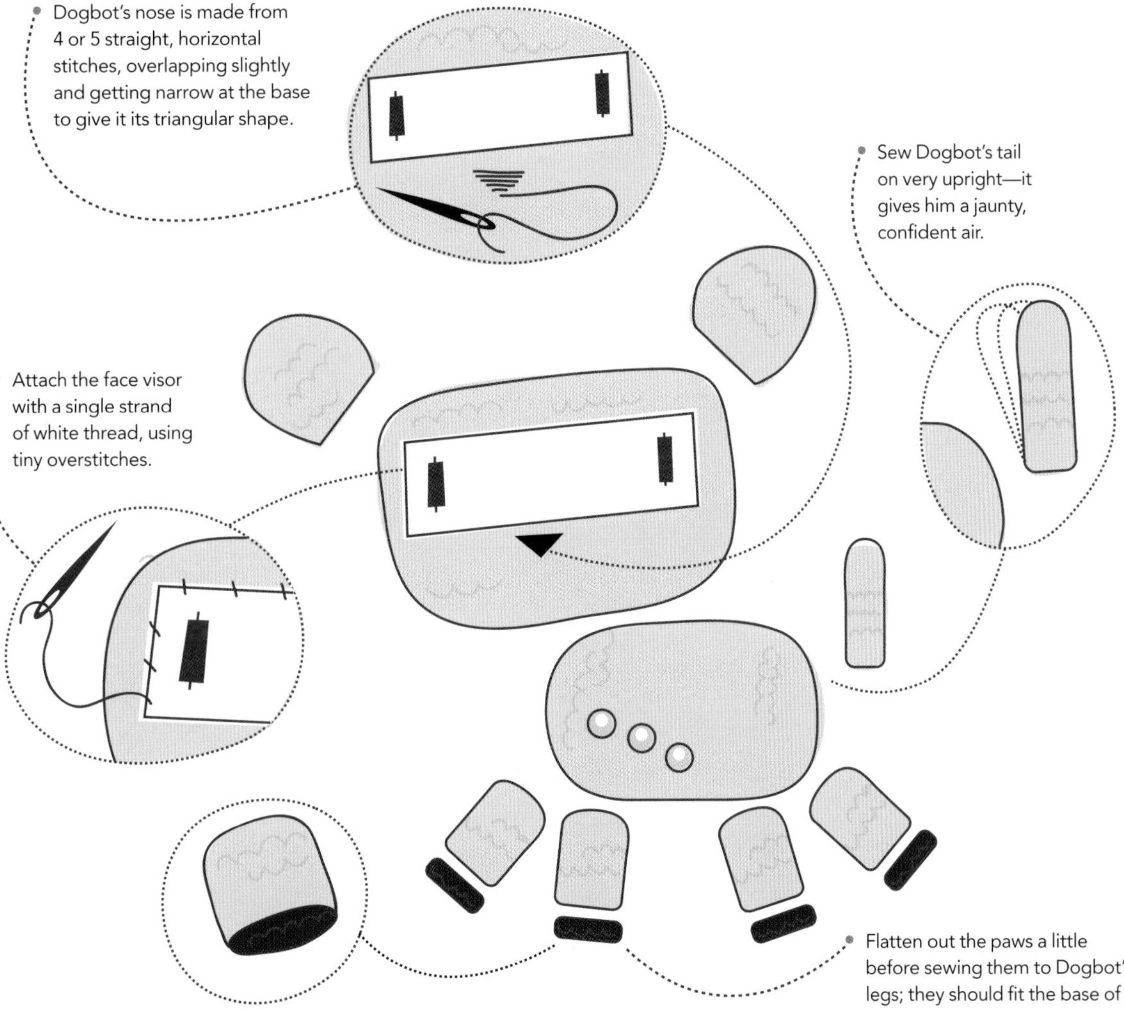

Flatten out the paws a little before sewing them to Dogbot's legs; they should fit the base of each leg neatly.

BOPBOT

This cool dude of the crobot world is dancing to a tune that only he can hear. He's big as these little creatures go, well over four inches, and his bold colors and assertive earphones tell you that he'll calmly deal with any obstacles that get in his way. Forget iTunes; just turn over your 'pod to this music-loving bot and he'll handle the all-important job of your selections.

YOU WILL NEED

- crochet hook, size C2 (2.75 mm)
- stitch marker or paper clip
- 1 yarn needle
- 1 embroidery needle
- 1 beading needle
- toy stuffing to stuff the bot
- blue yarn
- rust-colored yarn
- black yarn (for the headphones)
- gray yarn (for the headphones)
- black embroidery floss (1 strand)
- blue embroidery floss (1 strand)
- 2 black beads, about ⅛ inch (4 mm) in diameter
- 4 silver sequins
- 4 tiny clear beads to secure sequins in place
- 1 screw-clasp jewelry fastener
- 1 pen spring (dismantle a retractable ballpoint pen to obtain this)

SKILL LEVEL

TO MAKE BOPBOT

To make the head, using blue and rust-colored yarn

Start with blue yarn
Round 1 Start 6 sc in a magic ring (6)
Round 2 2 sc in each sc around (12)
Round 3 *2 sc in next sc, sc in next sc* repeat 6 times (18)
Round 4 *2 sc in next sc, sc in next 2 sc* repeat 6 times (24)
Rounds 5 to 12 sc in each sc around (24)

Change to rust-colored yarn
Rounds 13 to 15 sc in each sc around (24)

Change back to blue yarn
Rounds 16 to 18 sc in each sc around (24)

Change back to rust-colored yarn
Rounds 19 to 21 sc in each sc around (24)
Stuff firmly
sl st in next sc and tie off, leave long tail

To make the body, using blue yarn
Round 1 Start 6 sc in a magic ring (6)

ABBREVIATIONS: **ch** = *chain* **st** = *stitch* **sl st** = *slip stitch* **sc** = *single crochet* **hdc** = *half-double crochet* **sc dec** = *single crochet decrease (decrease over 2 stitches)* **blo** = *back loops only* *** = *repeat instructions between asterisks*

Round 2 2 sc in each sc around (12)
Round 3 *2 sc in next sc, sc in next sc*
repeat 6 times (18)
Round 4 *2 sc in next sc, sc in next 2 sc*
repeat 6 times (24)
sl st in next sc and tie off, weave in the end yarn

To make the arms, using blue and rust-colored yarn
Start with blue yarn
Round 1 Start 6 sc in a magic ring (6)
Round 2 *2 sc in next sc, sc in next 2 sc*
repeat twice (8)
Round 3 sc in each sc around (8)

Change to rust-colored yarn
Rounds 4 to 6 sc in each sc around (8)

Change back to blue yarn
Rounds 7 to 9 sc in each sc around (8)
Stuff a little
sl st in next sc and tie off, leave long tail
to attach to body
Make 2

To make the legs, using blue yarn
Round 1 Start 6 sc in a magic ring (6)
Round 2 2 sc in each sc around (12)
Round 3 in blo *sc in each sc around* (12)
Rounds 4 to 6 sc in each sc around (12)
Stuff firmly
sl st in next sc and tie off, leave long tail
to attach to body
Make 2

To make the headphones, using black yarn
Round 1 Start 6 sc in a magic ring (6)
Round 2 2 sc in each sc around (12)
Round 3 *2 sc in next sc, sc in next 3 sc*
repeat 3 times (15)
Round 4 sc in each sc around (15)
Round 5 *sc dec, sc in next 3 sc* repeat 3 times (12)
sl st in next sc and tie off, leave long tail
to sew to head
Stuff firmly
Make 2

To make the headphone cord, using gray yarn
ch 18
Tie off, leave long tail to attach to headphones

TO ASSEMBLE BOPBOT

- Sew Bopbot's head to his body using the tail of yarn left from crocheting. Stuff firmly before stitching closed.
- Use one strand of black floss to sew the black bead eyes in place on the face, and one strand of blue floss to stitch the mouth. Attach the pen spring using small overstitches at either end to secure it neatly.
- Use a beading needle threaded with a single strand of blue floss to add the beads and sequins in an asymmetric diamond shape on the front of the body. Thread the needle through the body, then thread on a sequin and a tiny clear bead. Thread the needle back through the central hole of the sequin and back through the body. The bead is larger than the hole in the sequin, so it will hold the sequin in place.
- Stuff the headphones and attach them to the head with tails of yarn left from crocheting. Unscrew the jewelry fastener and use one strand of black floss to sew one half of the clasp in the center of each headphone. Attach the cord to the headphones using leftover tails of yarn.
- Stuff Bopbot's arms and legs and attach them to his body with leftover yarn.
- Shape your crobot firmly with your fingers. You can angle the arms to make him look as though he's dancing.

BLUEPRINT

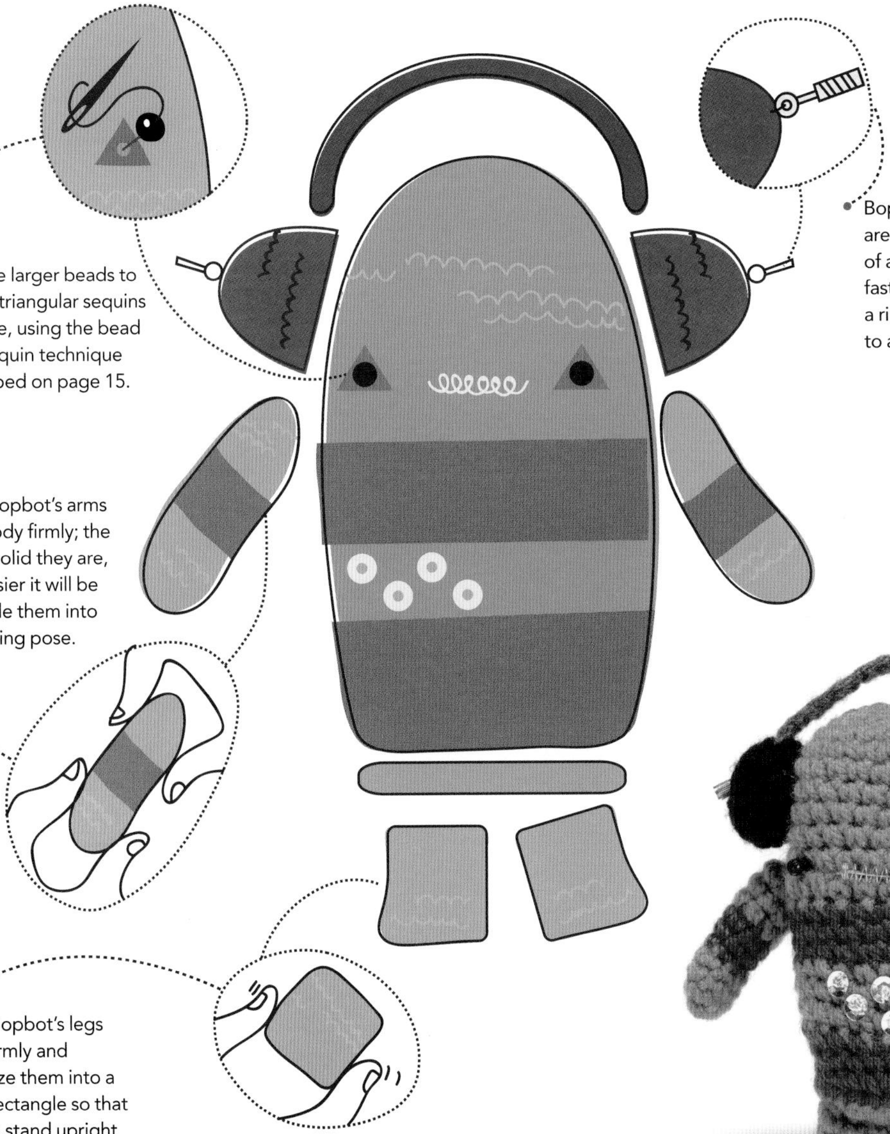

Use the larger beads to fix the triangular sequins in place, using the bead and sequin technique described on page 15.

Bopbot's headphones are finished with half of a screw jewelry fastener. The fixing has a ring to sew through to attach it.

Stuff Bopbot's arms and body firmly; the more solid they are, the easier it will be to angle them into a dancing pose.

Stuff Bopbot's legs very firmly and squeeze them into a neat rectangle so that he can stand upright without propping.

ZOMBIEBOT

Just like people, crobots can get into trouble, too. No one knows what kind of accident this little bot has been in, but it was clearly a bad one. Someone has patched him up, rather roughly, but he still needs a lot of care to nurse him back to health. Even his silver cladding is rough and discolored, and one of his arms is hanging by a crocheted thread. He'll be so grateful for peace and quiet that all you need to do is find him a calm corner to call home—he'll be your friend for life.

YOU WILL NEED

- crochet hook, size C2 (2.75 mm)
- stitch marker or paper clip
- 1 yarn needle
- 1 embroidery needle
- toy stuffing to stuff the bot
- textured beige yarn (a slightly spotty, tweedy texture is best to give your crobot an authentically distressed appearance)
- black embroidery floss (2 strands)
- beige embroidery floss (1 strand)
- 3 medium-sized screws, ¾ inch (15 mm) long
- 1 small nail
- 2 small gray shirt buttons (mismatched buttons will give Zombiebot an even more disheveled look)
- 2 small springs (dismantle 2 retractable ballpoint pens to obtain these)

SKILL LEVEL

TO MAKE ZOMBIEBOT

To make the head, using spotty beige yarn

Round 1 Start 6 sc in a magic ring (6)
Round 2 2 sc in each sc around (12)
Round 3 *2 sc in next sc, sc in next sc* repeat 6 times (18)
Round 4 *2 sc in next sc, sc in next 2 sc* repeat 6 times (24)
Round 5 *2 sc in next sc, sc in next 3 sc* repeat 6 times (30)
Rounds 6 to 10 sc in each sc around (30)
Round 11 *sc dec, sc in next 3 sc* repeat 6 times (24)
Round 12 *sc dec, sc in next 2 sc* repeat 6 times (18)
Round 13 *sc in next sc, sc dec* repeat 6 times (12)
Stuff firmly
sl st in next sc and tie off, leave long tail to attach to body

To make the body, using spotty beige yarn

Round 1 Start 6 sc in a magic ring (6)
Round 2 2 sc in each sc around (12)
Round 3 *2 sc in next sc, 1 sc in next sc* repeat 6 times (18)

ABBREVIATIONS: ch = *chain* **st** = *stitch* **sl st** = *slip stitch* **sc** = *single crochet* **hdc** = *half-double crochet* **sc dec** = *single crochet decrease (decrease over 2 stitches)* **blo** = *back loops only* * = *repeat instructions between asterisks*

Round 4 in blo, *sc in each sc around* (18)
Rounds 5 to 11 sc in each sc around (18)
Stuff firmly
sl st in next sc and tie off, weave in the end yarn

To make the arms, using spotty beige yarn
Round 1 Start 4 sc in a magic ring (4)
Round 2 *2 sc in next sc, sc in next sc* repeat twice (6)
Rounds 3 to 5 sc in each sc around (6)
sl st in next sc and tie off, leave long tail to sew to body
Stuff lightly
Make 2

To make the legs, using spotty beige yarn
Round 1 Start 6 sc in a magic ring (6)
Round 2 *2 sc in next sc, sc in next 2 sc* repeat twice (8)
Round 3 in blo, *sc dec, sc in next 2 sc* repeat twice (6)
Rounds 4 to 6 sc in each sc around (6)
sl st in next sc and tie off, leave long tail to sew to body
Stuff firmly
Make 2

To make the head, using spotty beige yarn
Round 1 Start 6 sc in a magic ring (6)
Round 2 2 sc in each sc around (12)
Round 3 *2 sc in next sc, sc in next sc* repeat 6 times (18)
Round 4 *2 sc in next sc, sc in next 2 sc* repeat 6 times (24)
Round 5 *2 sc in next sc, sc in next 3 sc* repeat 6 times (30)
Rounds 6 to 10 sc in each sc around (30)
Round 11 *sc dec, sc in next 3 sc* repeat 6 times (24)
Round 12 *sc dec, sc in next 2 sc* repeat 6 times (18)
Round 13 *sc in next sc, sc dec* repeat 6 times (12)
Stuff firmly
sl st in next sc and tie off, leave long tail to attach to body

To make the body, using spotty beige yarn
Round 1 Start 6 sc in a magic ring (6)
Round 2 2 sc in each sc around (12)
Round 3 *2 sc in next sc, 1 sc in next sc* repeat 6 times (18)
Round 4 in blo, *sc in each sc around* (18)
Rounds 5 to 11 sc in each sc around (18)
Stuff firmly
sl st in next sc and tie off, weave in the end yarn

To make the arms, using spotty beige yarn
Round 1 Start 4 sc in a magic ring (4)
Round 2 *2 sc in next sc, sc in next sc* repeat twice (6)
Rounds 3 to 5 sc in each sc around (6)
sl st in next sc and tie off, leave long tail to sew to body
Stuff lightly
Make 2

To make the legs, using spotty beige yarn
Round 1 Start 6 sc in a magic ring (6)
Round 2 *2 sc in next sc, sc in next 2 sc* repeat twice (8)
Round 3 in blo, *sc dec, sc in next 2 sc* repeat twice (6)
Rounds 4 to 6 sc in each sc around (6)
sl st in next sc and tie off, leave long tail to sew to body
Stuff firmly
Make 2

TO ASSEMBLE ZOMBIEBOT

- Stuff the head firmly, thread an embroidery needle with two strands of black floss, and embroider two scars on Zombiebot's face. Use the photograph as a guide to place them, and make each from one long straight stitch with plenty of tiny straight stitches crossing it at right angles. Using one strand of beige floss, attach the left eye to the head.
- To make the damaged right eye, take one of the pen springs and sew one end of it to the face, using the beige floss. Attach the other end of the spring low on the face, then add a button at the lower end with several stitches, so that the eye appears to be dangling loosely on the cheek.

- Stuff the body firmly and embroider it with a scar in black floss, using the same process as the face scars. Attach the second spring across the upper left torso, stitching it on at each end with beige thread.
- Attach Zombiebot's head to his body using the leftover tail of yarn.
- Stuff the arms. Attach the left arm to the body by its tail of yarn. For the hanging right arm, leave the top open with some stuffing protruding, and attach it on a length of yarn about one-half inch long, leaving it hanging loosely against Zombiebot's side.
- Stuff the legs. Embroider a tiny scar on the right leg, and attach both legs to the body with the tails of yarn left over from crocheting.
- Using the photograph as a reference, gently press the screws and the nail into position on Zombiebot's head.

BLUEPRINT

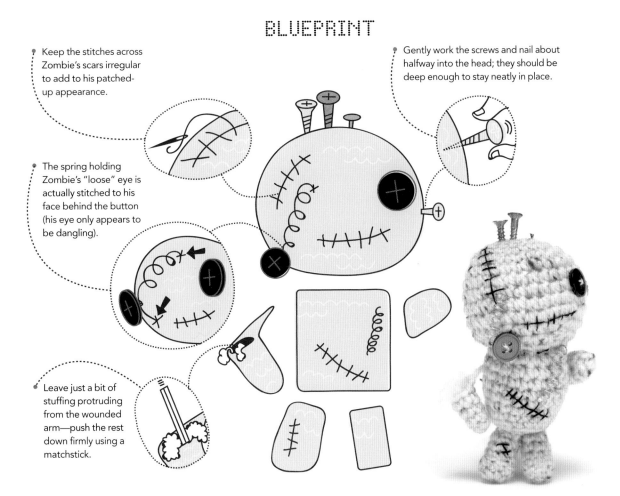

Keep the stitches across Zombie's scars irregular to add to his patched-up appearance.

Gently work the screws and nail about halfway into the head; they should be deep enough to stay neatly in place.

The spring holding Zombie's "loose" eye is actually stitched to his face behind the button (his eye only appears to be dangling).

Leave just a bit of stuffing protruding from the wounded arm—push the rest down firmly using a matchstick.

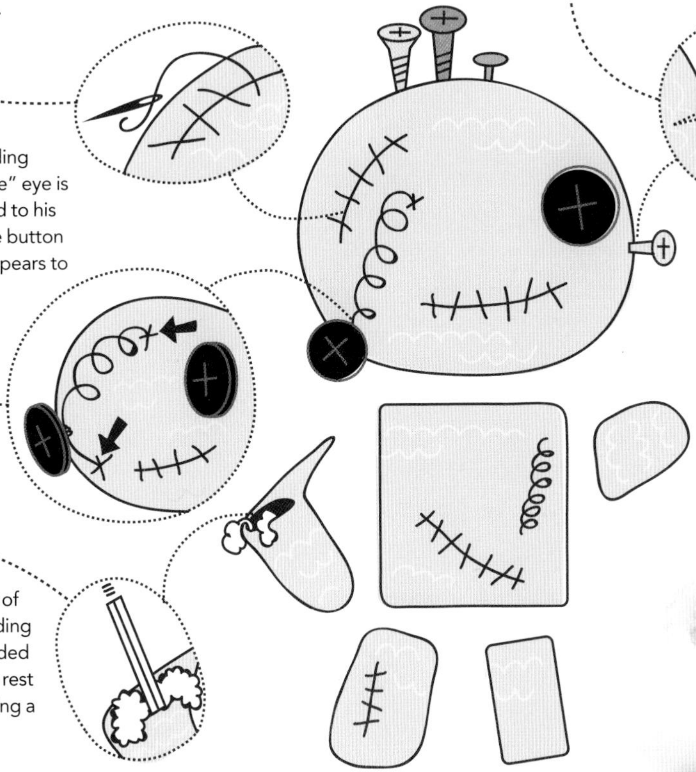

MECHANOBOT

Mechanobot is a hard worker. His huge rectangular head contains enough wiring for him to remember how everything works and how it can be fixed when it's broken. And he's willing to help, whatever the problem. His chocolate-mint color combination is set off by little metal details, although most hail from the haberdashery counter rather than the hardware store.

YOU WILL NEED

- crochet hook, size C2 (2.75 mm)
- stitch marker or paper clip
- 1 yarn needle
- 1 embroidery needle
- 1 beading needle
- toy stuffing to stuff the bot
- chocolate-brown yarn
- mint-green yarn
- black embroidery floss (2 strands)
- chocolate-brown embroidery floss (1 strand)
- 2 black sequins (for the eyes)
- 2 brooch bar fasteners (available in craft stores)
- 1 small brooch-back fastener (available in craft stores)
- 2 pen springs (dismantle 2 retractable ballpoint pens to obtain these)
- 1 screw, ¾ inch (15 mm) long
- 3 small clear beads
- 6 medium silver snap fasteners

SKILL LEVEL

TO MAKE MECHANOBOT

To make the face and front of the head, using mint-green and chocolate-brown yarn
Start with green yarn
Row 1 ch 16, sc in 2nd ch from hook and in each ch across (15) ch 1 and turn
Rows 2 to 5 sc in each sc across (15) ch 1 and turn
Row 6 sc in next 14 sc, 3 sc in last sc (17)
Work a round of single crochet on the rectangle, going down left side
sc in next 3 sc, 3 sc in next sc (2nd corner)
sc in next 12 sc, 3 sc in next sc (3rd corner)
sc in next 3 sc, 2 sc in next sc (4th corner) (43)

Change to brown yarn
Work in the round
Round 7 sc in each sc around (43)
Round 8 in blo *sc in each sc around* (43)
Rounds 9 to 12 sc in each sc around (43)
sl st in next sc and tie off, leave long tail to sew to back of the head

ABBREVIATIONS: ch = *chain* **st** = *stitch* **sl st** = *slip stitch* **sc** = *single crochet* **hdc** = *half-double crochet* **sc dec** = *single crochet decrease (decrease over 2 stitches)* **blo** = *back loops only* ***** = *repeat instructions between asterisks*

To make the back of the head, using chocolate-brown yarn
Follow the pattern for the front of the head up to end of row 6 (you have 43 sc)

To make the body, using chocolate-brown yarn
Round 1 Start 6 sc in a magic ring (6)
Round 2 2 sc in each sc around (12)
Round 3 *2 sc in next sc, sc in next sc* repeat 6 times (18)
Round 4 in back loops only *sc in each sc around* (18)
Rounds 5 to 9 sc in each sc around (18)
Stuff firmly
sl st in next sc and tie off, leave long tail to attach to head

TO ASSEMBLE MECHANOBOT

- Using two strands of black floss, sew the sequins in position on the front of the face. Next embroider the mouth and eyebrows, checking the photograph for placement. The mouth is simply one long, single straight stitch and the eyebrows are one small straight stitch each.
- Attach the face to the back of the head using the tail of yarn left over from crocheting. Stuff firmly before closing up.
- Thread a needle with one strand of brown floss and sew the large brooch backs to the sides of the head to make Mechanobot's ears. Stitch the small brooch back on top of the head to make a receiver.
- Stuff the body firmly and close up. Using a beading needle with one strand of brown floss, sew the beads in a row along Mechanobot's body. Add the screw to the center of the body with a few stitches. Use a single strand of brown floss to sew the pen springs onto the body, bending them in from the sides so it looks as though Mechanobot has a firm grip on the screw. Sew the springs down with a few stitches at each end.
- Mechanobot's legs are made from little stacks of press fasteners. Stack three fasteners on top of one another and use two strands of brown floss to sew through them all, then stitch to the body around the edges. Repeat for the second leg.
- Finally, attach Mechanobot's head to his body using the leftover tail of yarn.

BLUEPRINT

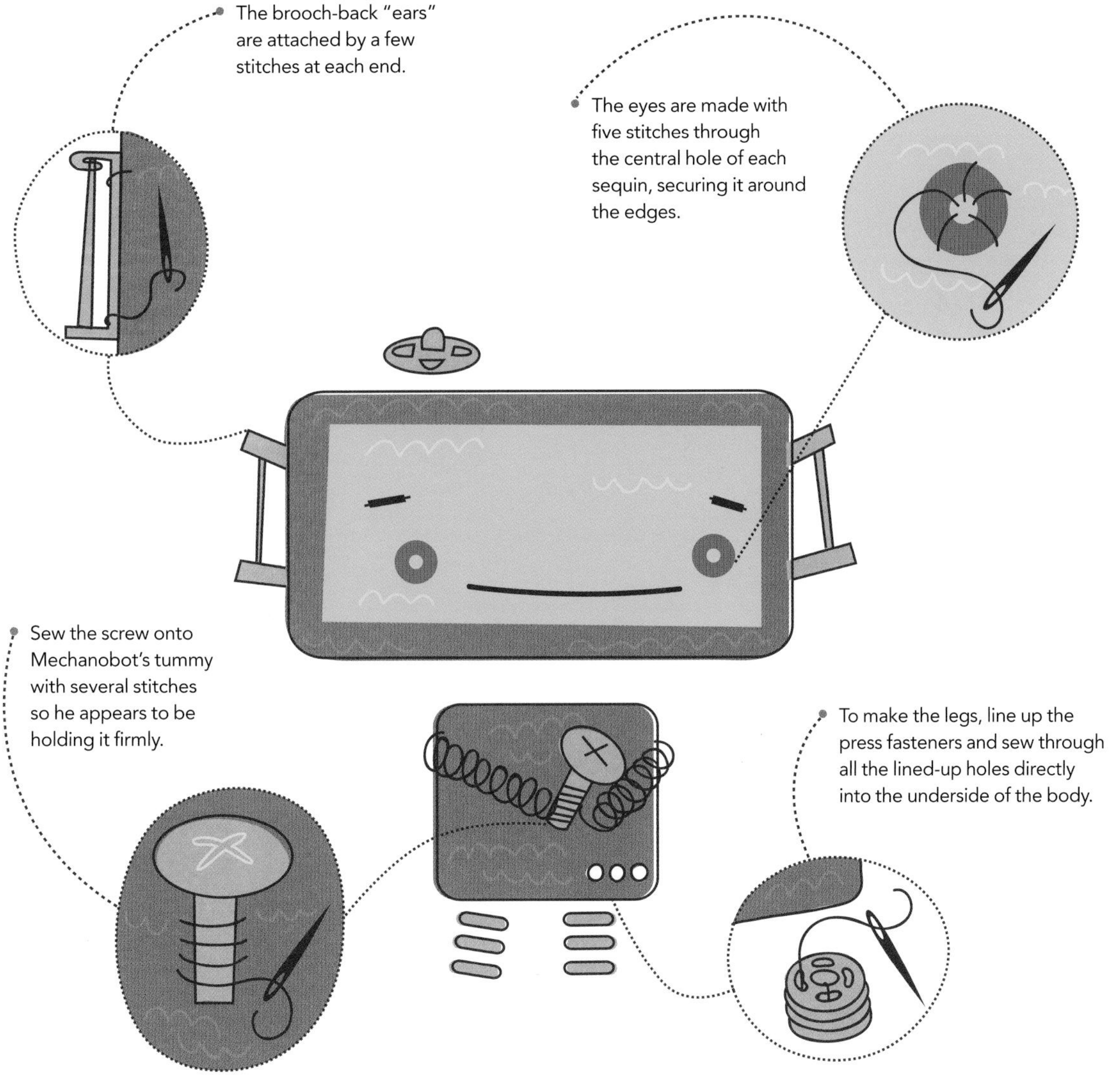
The brooch-back "ears" are attached by a few stitches at each end.
The eyes are made with five stitches through the central hole of each sequin, securing it around the edges.
Sew the screw onto Mechanobot's tummy with several stitches so he appears to be holding it firmly.
To make the legs, line up the press fasteners and sew through all the lined-up holes directly into the underside of the body.

RETROBOT

If you've ever enjoyed a vintage movie featuring robots, then Retrobot may have an oddly familiar look. His more-than-passing resemblance to Robbie the Robot, star of comics from the 1950s, combined with his red, black, and orange color scheme, gives him old-fashioned appeal. Some modern crobots have few visible controls, but Retrobot has plenty of reassuring buttons and switches on his outer casing.

YOU WILL NEED

- crochet hook, size C2 (2.75 mm)
- stitch marker or paper clip
- 1 yarn needle
- 1 embroidery needle
- 1 beading needle
- toy stuffing to stuff the bot
- cherry-colored yarn
- black yarn
- bright orange yarn
- scrap of white felt (for the eye panel)
- white embroidery floss (1 strand)
- green embroidery floss (1 strand)
- orange embroidery floss (1 strand)
- cherry-red embroidery floss (1 strand)
- metallic gray embroidery floss (1 strand)
- 5 green beads, ⅛ inch (4 mm) in diameter
- 2 red sequins
- 3 green sequins
- 9 green bugle beads, ¼ inch (7 mm) long
- 4 small washers
- 1 small screw
- 2 small valves (for the arms)

SKILL LEVEL

TO MAKE RETROBOT

To make the head, using cherry-colored yarn

Round 1 Start 6 sc in a magic ring (6)
Do not pull the yarn too tightly, as you will need to add a screw on top of his head
Round 2 2 sc in each sc around (12)
Round 3 *2 sc in next sc, sc in next sc* repeat 6 times (18)
Round 4 *2 sc in next sc, sc in next 2 sc* repeat 6 times (24)
Rounds 5 to 9 sc in each sc around (24)
sl st in next sc and tie off, weave in the end yarn

To make the lower body, using black yarn

Same as head up to the end of row 9

ABBREVIATIONS: **ch** = *chain* **st** = *stitch* **sl st** = *slip stitch* **sc** = *single crochet* **hdc** = *half-double crochet* **sc dec** = *single crochet decrease (decrease over 2 stitches)* **blo** = *back loops only* * = *repeat instructions between asterisks*

Change to orange yarn
Round 10 sc in each sc around (24)
sl st in next sc and tie off, leave long tail to sew to head

To make the legs, using orange yarn
Round 1 Start 4 sc in a magic ring (4)
Round 2 *2 sc in next sc, sc in next sc* repeat twice (6)
Round 3 in blo *sc in each sc around* (6)
Round 4 and 5 sc in each sc around (6)
Stuff a little
sl st in next sc and tie off, leave long tail to attach to body
Make 2

To make the feet, using cherry-colored yarn
Round 1 Start 6 sc in a magic ring (6)
Round 2 *2 sc in next sc, sc in next 2 sc* repeat twice (8)
Sl st in next sc and tie off, weave in the end yarn
Make 2

TO ASSEMBLE RETROBOT

- Stuff the head and body firmly, then sew them together around the center with the tail of leftover orange yarn. Just before closing the gap, add a little more stuffing so that Retrobot is a good solid egg shape. Thread a needle with orange yarn and backstitch a straight line down the center of Retrobot's belly.
- Cut a narrow rectangular piece of white felt for the eye visor, comparing it to the photograph and Retrobot's body to ensure that it is the right size. Attach the eyes to the felt by threading a beading needle with one strand of green floss, stitching it through the felt in the position of the first eye, then threading on one red sequin followed by a green bead. Feed the needle back through the center hole of the sequin (the bead will hold it in place) and back through the felt. Finish off at the back. Repeat for the second eye. When both eyes are in place, thread an embroidery needle with one strand of white floss and attach the eye visor to the face with tiny overstitches.
- Thread the beading needle with a single strand of cherry-red floss and sew three green bugle beads onto Retrobot's forehead, as shown in the photograph.
- Using a single strand of metallic gray floss, sew the washers in place on Retrobot's head— they're a combination of his ears and receivers. Gently press the screw halfway into the center point at the crown of Retrobot's head.
- Still using a strand of metallic gray floss, sew the two remaining washers into place on the body. Thread the beading needle with one strand of green floss and add the beads and sequins to the orange line on Retrobot's tummy.
- Stuff the legs firmly, then use the beading needle and one strand of orange floss to sew three green bugle beads onto each one. Attach the legs to the body with leftover tails of yarn.
- Use a piece of cherry-colored yarn to stitch the feet to the base of the legs.
- Using one strand of black floss, sew on the little valves to make Retrobot's arms.

BLUEPRINT

You will find tiny valves and other "robotic" accessories in modelmaking stores. Look for ones with a ring or hole at one end so they'll be easy to attach.

Use a single strand of white floss and tiny overstitches to attach Retrobot's eye visor to his face.

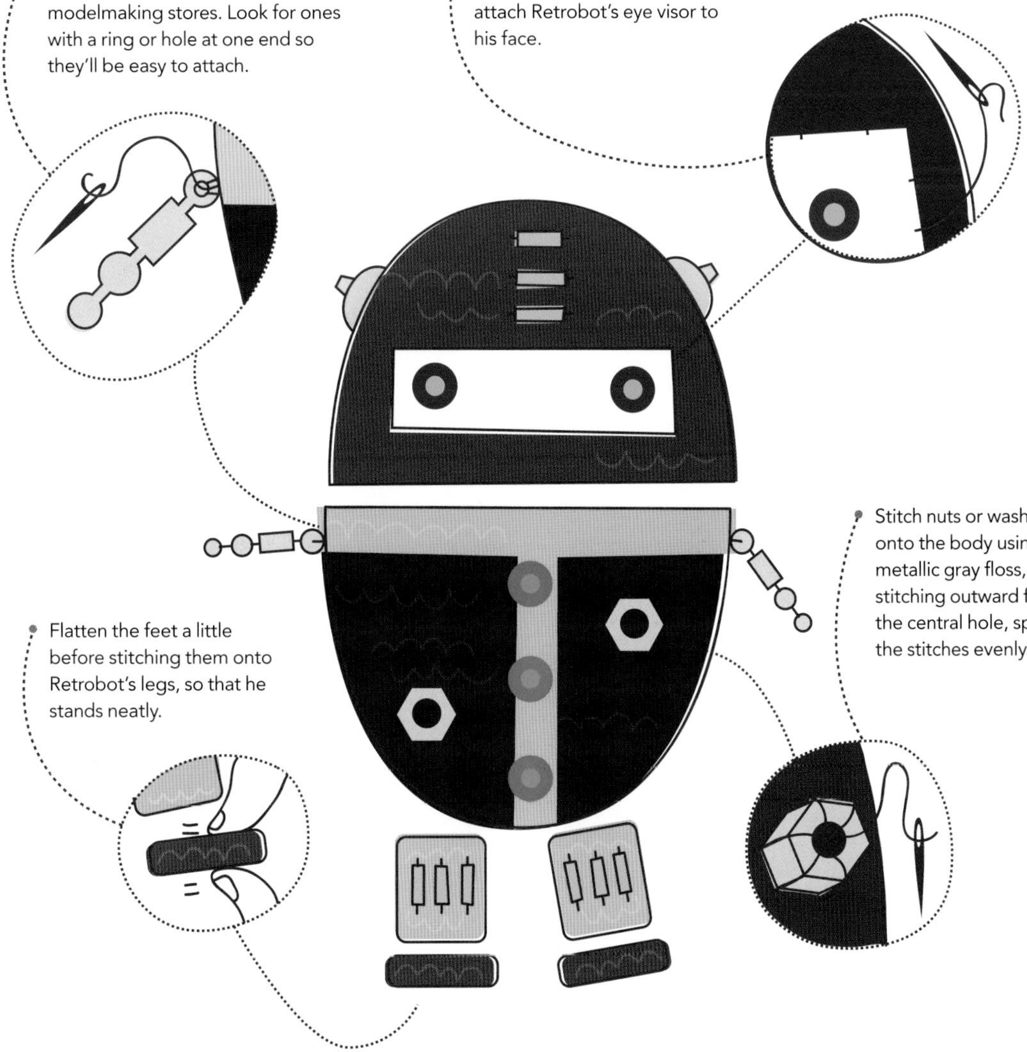

Stitch nuts or washers onto the body using metallic gray floss, and stitching outward from the central hole, spacing the stitches evenly.

Flatten the feet a little before stitching them onto Retrobot's legs, so that he stands neatly.

BOXBOT

Boxbot isn't much larger than a matchbox, although he stands firmly upright on two button legs. His surprised expression and many small embellishments give him a typical crobot charm, but it's not quite obvious what his robotic job should be. As his creator and owner, you may have to invent a useful role for him.

YOU WILL NEED

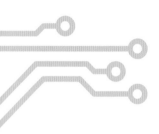

- crochet hook, size C2 (2.75 mm)
- stitch marker or paper clip
- 1 yarn needle
- 1 embroidery needle
- 1 beading needle
- toy stuffing to stuff the bot
- brown yarn
- green yarn
- red yarn
- scrap of gray felt
- gray embroidery floss (1 strand)
- red embroidery floss (1 strand)
- green embroidery floss (1 strand)
- 6 dark beads, ⅛ inch (4 mm) in diameter
- 2 red sequins
- 6 green bugle beads, ¼ inch (7 mm) long
- 6 yellow bugle beads, ¼ inch (7 mm) long
- 2 black bugle beads, ¼ inch (7 mm) long
- 1 red bugle bead, ¼ inch (7 mm) long
- 2 small black press fasteners (for the eyes)
- 2 red sequins
- 2 tiny red beads
- 1 brooch bar fastener (available at craft stores)
- 6 tiny yellow beads
- 2 screws, ¾ inch (15 mm) long
- 1 small faceted nut, about ⅖ inch (1 cm) in diameter
- 2 medium-sized dark buttons (for the feet)

SKILL LEVEL

TO MAKE BOXBOT

To make the head and body, using brown, red, and green yarn

Row 1 ch 10, sc in 2nd ch from hook and in each ch across (9) ch 1 and turn
Rows 2 to 6 sc in each sc across (9) ch 1 and turn
Row 7 sc in each sc across and at the end of the row ch 1 (10)

Work a round of single crochet on the square, going down left side
sc in next 5 sc, 3 sc in next sc (2nd corner)
sc in next 6 sc, 3 sc in next sc (3nd corner)
sc in next 5 sc (4th corner) (32)

ABBREVIATIONS: **ch** = *chain* **st** = *stitch* **sl st** = *slip stitch* **sc** = *single crochet* **hdc** = *half-double crochet* **sc dec** = *single crochet decrease (decrease over 2 stitches)* **blo** = *back loops only* ***** = *repeat instructions between asterisks*

Now working in blo
sc in next 8 sc and skip one
sc in next 6 sc and skip one
sc in next 8 sc and skip one
sc in next 6 sc and skip one (28)
Now working in the round, still with brown yarn
Rounds 1 to 6 sc in each sc around (28)

Change to red yarn
Rounds 7 and 8 sc in each sc around (28)

Change to green yarn
Rounds 9 to 13 sc in each sc around (28)
sl st in next sc and tie off, weave in the end yarn

To make the base, using green yarn
Start in the same way as the head, repeat up to the end of row 7 (you now have 32 sc)
sl st in next sc and tie off, leave long tail to sew to head

TO ASSEMBLE BOXBOT

- Start by stuffing the body quite firmly. Sew the base to the body using the leftover tail of yarn. (Note: There are 28 sc around for the body and 32 sc for the base, so skip one stitch of the bottom piece at each corner as you sew it on.) Shape Boxbot to a nice even shape, with a flat top to his head.
- Cut a small rectangle of gray felt for Boxbot's face, then place it against his body and compare to the photograph to ensure that it will fit. Thread the beading needle with one strand of gray floss and sew Boxbot's snap fastener eyes into place on the felt. Then add his eyebrows, which are made with black bugle beads sewn on at a jaunty angle. Finally, add his mouth, which is a red bugle bead sewn on horizontally between the eyes.
- Stitch the face onto Boxbot's head, using a single strand of gray floss and small overstitches. Gently push a screw halfway into each side of Boxbot's head, making sure that they are positioned evenly. Then sew the nut to the top of Boxbot's head using a single strand of gray floss.
- Thread the beading needle with one strand of red floss and sew six bugle beads vertically onto the red stripe on the body, alternating green and gold beads. Sew the red sequins onto the body, stitching through the center hole and making five stitches around the edge.
- Thread the beading needle with one strand of green floss and sew three dark beads down one of Boxbot's sides. Repeat on the other side. Next attach the brooch bar fastener to the center of the body with a few stitches. Add a row of small yellow beads below the brooch pin, referring to the photograph for placement.
- Use green yarn to sew the two buttons onto Boxbot's base: They will serve as his short but practical legs.

BLUEPRINT

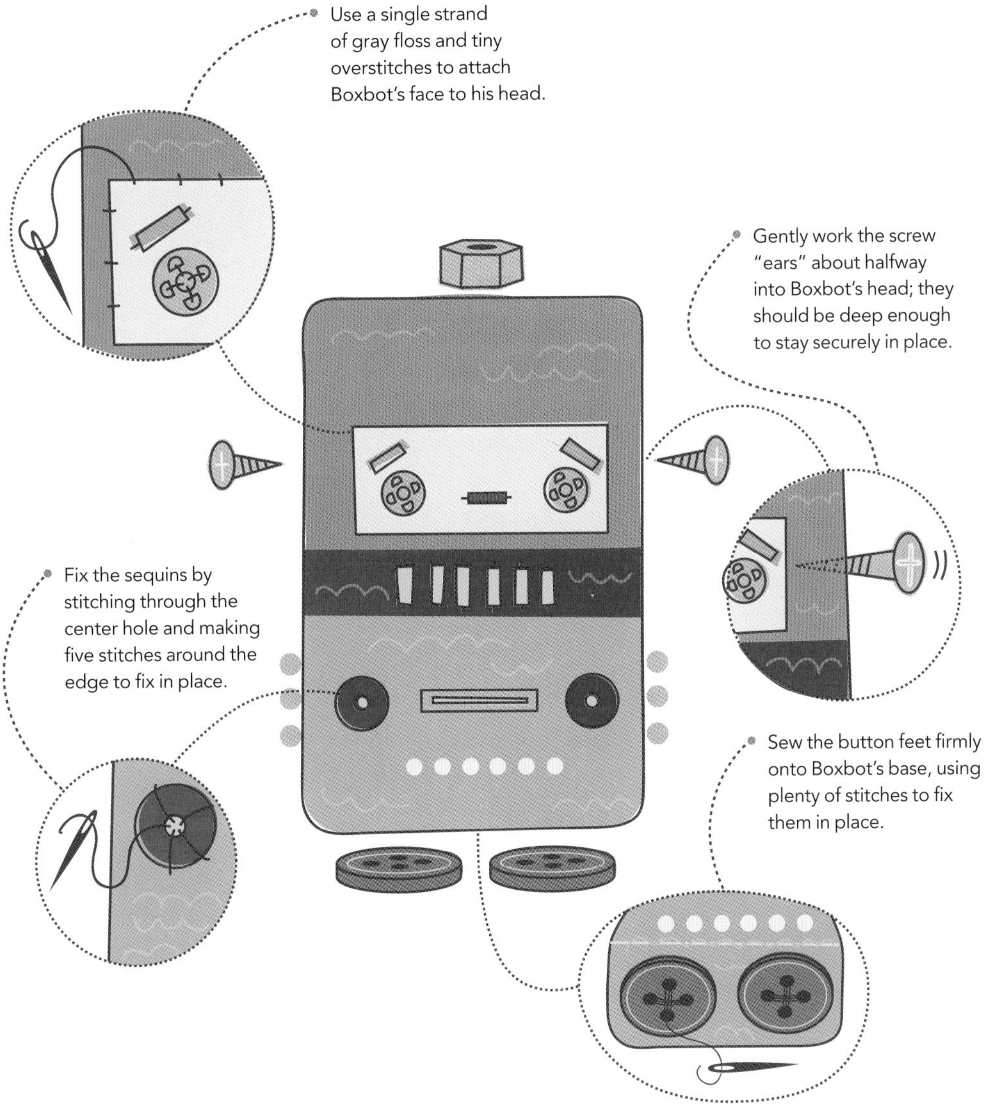
Use a single strand of gray floss and tiny overstitches to attach Boxbot's face to his head.
Gently work the screw "ears" about halfway into Boxbot's head; they should be deep enough to stay securely in place.
Fix the sequins by stitching through the center hole and making five stitches around the edge to fix in place.
Sew the button feet firmly onto Boxbot's base, using plenty of stitches to fix them in place.

BIGBOT

Bigbot has a positively threatening appearance—for a crobot, that is. His antennae are made from trembling springs, his fuel dial hovers around the halfway mark, and his expression is inscrutable. Is that big claw-like arm raised in a salute or a more forceful gesture? We can only guess, but his cheerful orange-and-green color combination, sequin adornments, and stubby little fingers suggest that this desktop guardian is friendly enough.

YOU WILL NEED

- crochet hook, size C2 (2.75 mm)
- stitch marker or paper clip
- 1 yarn needle
- 1 embroidery needle
- 1 beading needle
- toy stuffing to stuff the bot
- orange yarn
- green yarn
- gray yarn
- black, white, and red embroidery floss
- gray embroidery floss
- 2 black sequins
- tiny scrap of white felt
- 1 gold sequin and one tiny black bead
- 2 silver sequins
- 2 clear beads to secure the sequins in place
- 2 pen springs (dismantle 2 retractable ballpoint pens to obtain these)

SKILL LEVEL

✱✱

TO MAKE BIGBOT

To make the body, using orange yarn

Row 1 ch 14, sc in 2nd ch from hook and in each ch across (13) ch 1 and turn
Rows 2 to 9 sc in each sc across (13) ch 1 and turn
Row 10 12 sc across, 3 sc in last sc (15)

Work a round of single crochet on the rectangle, going down left side
sc 7, 3 sc in last sc (2nd corner)
sc 11, 3 sc in last sc (3rd corner)
sc 7, 3 sc in last sc (4th corner)
sl st in next sc and tie off, weave in the end yarn (49)
Make 2

Sides in one piece

Row 1 ch 8, sc in 2nd ch from hook and in each ch across (7) ch 1 and turn
Rows 2 to 10 sc in each sc across (7) ch 1 and turn
Row 11 in blo, sc in each sc across (7) ch 1 and turn
Rows 12 to 22 sc in each sc across (7) ch 1 and turn
Row 23 in blo, sc in each sc across (7) ch 1 and turn
Rows 24 to 32 sc in each sc across (7) ch 1 and turn

ABBREVIATIONS: **ch** = *chain* **st** = *stitch* **sl st** = *slip stitch* **sc** = *single crochet* **hdc** = *half-double crochet* **sc dec** = *single crochet decrease (decrease over 2 stitches)* **blo** = *back loops only* * = *repeat instructions between asterisks*

Row 33 in blo, sc in each sc across (7) ch 1 and turn
Rows 34 to 44 sc in each sc across (7) and tie off, weave in the end yarn

To make the legs, using orange and gray yarn
Start with orange yarn
Round 1 Start 6 sc in a magic ring (6)
Round 2 2 sc in each sc (12)
Round 3 *2 sc in next sc, sc in next sc* repeat 6 times (18)
Round 4 blo just for this round *sc dec, sc in next sc* repeat 6 times (12)
Round 5 *sc dec, sc in next 4 sc* repeat twice (10)
Round 6 to 7 sc around (10)

Change to gray yarn
Round 8 *2 sc in next sc, sc in next 4 sc* repeat twice (12)
Round 9 *2 sc in next sc, sc in next sc* repeat 6 times (18)
Round 10 decrease around (9)

Change to orange yarn
Rounds 11 to 12 sc around (9)
sl st in next sc and tie off, leave long tail
Make 2

To make the arms, using green, gray, and orange yarn
Start with green yarn
Round 1 Start 6 sc in a magic ring (6)
Round 2 2 sc in each sc around (12)
Round 3 *2 sc in next sc, 1 sc in next sc* repeat 6 times (18)
Rounds 4 to 5 sc in each sc around (18)
Round 6 *sc dec, sc in next sc* repeat 6 times (12)
Round 7 decrease around (6)

Change to orange yarn
Round 8 *2 sc in next sc, sc in next 2 sc* repeat twice (8)
Rounds 9 to 12 sc around (8)

Change to gray yarn
Round 13 sc around (8)

Change to green yarn
Round 14 *2 sc in next sc, sc in next sc* repeat 4 times (12)
Round 15 *hdc dec, hdc in next 4 sc* repeat twice (10)
sl st in next sc and tie off, weave in the end yarn
Make 2

To make the leg trimmings, using green yarn
Round 1 Start 4 sc in a magic ring (4)
Round 2 2 sc in each sc (8)
Round 3 blo sc around (8)
Round 4 *sc dec, sc in next 2 sc* repeat twice (6)
Stuff firmly
sl st in next sc and tie off, leave long tail
Make 2

TO ASSEMBLE BIGBOT

- Embroider the face on the front panel before assembling the body. Sew on the sequin eyes using one strand of black floss and placing them carefully. Embroider the mouth between the eyes, starting with two strands of white floss and making a rectangular shape with three or four long horizontal stitches. Change to black floss. Use tiny stitches to outline the edges of the mouth, then make a few tiny vertical stitches over the white area to define the teeth.
- Cut a little semicircle of white felt for Bigbot's control panel. With two strands of black floss, use straight stitches to embroider the fuel gauge. With two strands of red, straight stitch the dial needle. Overstitch the switch onto Bigbot with one strand of white.
- Add a gold sequin at the base of the control panel and secure it in place with a black bead. Add two silver sequins for switches on Bigbot's front, using one strand of gray thread and securing them with clear beads.

- Sew up the pieces to form the body, using orange yarn, and stuff firmly before closing up. Stuff the arms and attach to the body with tails of yarn. To add Bigbot's fingers, use a yarn needle and green yarn to make three French knots on each hand.
- Stuff the boot trimmings and attach them to the legs, then sew the legs onto the body with the leftover tails of yarn.
- You can either let the arms rest alongside the body or shape the right arm so it is making a robot salute in the air.
- Finally, use gray thread to attach the spring antennae on top of Bigbot's head with two or three tiny stitches.

BLUEPRINT

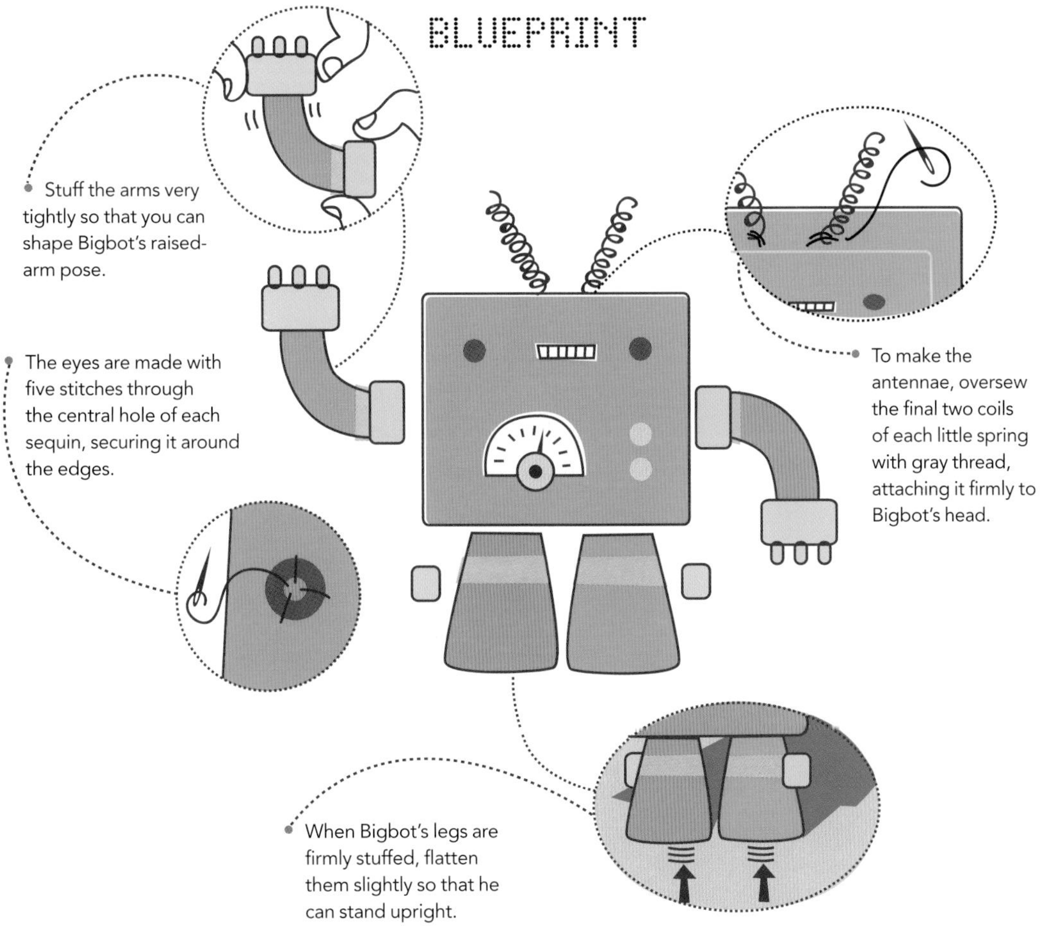
Stuff the arms very tightly so that you can shape Bigbot's raised-arm pose.
The eyes are made with five stitches through the central hole of each sequin, securing it around the edges.
To make the antennae, oversew the final two coils of each little spring with gray thread, attaching it firmly to Bigbot's head.
When Bigbot's legs are firmly stuffed, flatten them slightly so that he can stand upright.

BABYBOT

This juvenile robot still has a baby face, with long eyelashes and raised metallic eyebrows giving him a surprised expression. His square little head and body, the control panel on his front, and his three red receivers, however, make him a full-fledged robot. Embroider the face and the embellishments before assembling Babybot. A small metallic zigzag closure up his back adds the finishing touch.

YOU WILL NEED

- crochet hook, size C2 (2.75) mm
- stitch marker or paper clip
- 1 yarn needle
- 1 embroidery needle
- toy stuffing to stuff the bot
- gray yarn (for main head, body, arms, and legs)
- white yarn
- red yarn
- black embroidery floss
- metallic gray embroidery floss
- scrap of white felt (for the control panel)
- white sewing thread

SKILL LEVEL

TO MAKE BABYBOT

To make the head, using gray and white yarn

Back with gray yarn

Row 1 ch 10, sc in 2nd ch from hook and in each ch across (9) ch 1 and turn

Rows 2 to 6 sc in each sc across (9) ch 1 and turn

Row 7 sc in next 8 sc, 3 sc in last sc (11)

Work a round of single crochet on the square, going down left side

sc in next 5 sc, 3 sc in next sc (2nd corner)

sc in next 7 sc, 3 sc in next sc (3rd corner)

sc in next 5 sc, 3 sc in next sc (4th corner) (37)

sl st in next sc and tie off, weave in the end yarn

Front with white and gray yarn

Rows 1 to 6 with white yarn as back of the head (9)

Row 7 change to gray as back of the head (37)

Sides with gray yarn

Row 1 ch 6, sc in 2nd ch from hook and in each ch across (5) ch 1 and turn

Rows 2 to 8 sc in each sc across (5) ch 1 and turn

Row 9 in blo, sc in each sc across (5) ch 1 and turn

Rows 10 to 18 sc in each sc across (5) ch 1 and turn

Row 19 in blo, sc in each sc across (5) ch 1 and turn

Rows 20 to 25 sc in each sc across (5) ch 1 and turn

Tie off, weave in the end yarn

To make the body, using gray yarn

Back and front

Row 1 ch 6, sc in 2nd ch from hook and in each ch across (5) ch 1 and turn

Rows 2 to 3 sc in each sc across (5)

At the end of each row ch 1 and turn

Row 4 sc in next 4 sc, 3 sc in last sc (7)

ABBREVIATIONS: **ch** = *chain* **st** = *stitch* **sl st** = *slip stitch* **sc** = *single crochet* **hdc** = *half-double crochet* **sc dec** = *single crochet decrease (decrease over 2 stitches)* **blo** = *back loops only* ***** = *repeat instructions between asterisks*

Now work a round of single crochet on your square, going down left side
sc in next 1 sc, 3 sc in next sc (2nd corner)
sc in next 3 sc, 3 sc in next sc (3rd corner)
sc in next 3 sc (4th corner)
sl st in next sc and tie off, weave in the end yarn

Sides
Row 1 ch 5, sc in 2nd ch from hook and in each ch across (4) ch 1 and turn
Rows 2 to 5 sc in each sc across (4) ch 1 and turn
Row 6 in blo, sc in each sc across (4) ch 1 and turn
Rows 7 to 11 sc in each sc across (4) ch 1 and turn
Row 12 in blo, sc in each sc across (4) ch 1 and turn
Rows 13 to 15 sc in each sc across (4) ch 1 and turn
Row 16 in blo, sc in each sc across (4) ch 1 and turn
Rows 17 to 21 sc in each sc across (4)
Tie off, weave in the end yarn

To make the ears/receivers, using red yarn
Round 1 Start 6 sc in a magic ring (6)
Round 2 2 sc in each sc (12)
Round 3 in blo, sc around (12)
Round 4 *sc dec, sc in next 4 sc* repeat twice (10)
sl st in next sc and tie off, leave long tail
Stuff firmly
Make 3

To make the arms, using gray yarn
Round 1 Start 4 sc in a magic ring (4)
Round 2 2 sc in each sc (8)
Round 3 sc around (8)
Round 4 sc around (8)
Stuff
Round 5 sc dec, sc, sc dec, sc, sc dec (5)
Round 6 2 sc in each sc (10)
Round 7 *2 sc in next sc, sc in next 4 sc* repeat twice (12)
Round 8 sc around (12)
Stuff
Round 9 sc dec around (6)
Round 10 sc dec around
sl st in next sc and tie off, leaving long tail to close up
Make 2

To make the feet, using gray yarn
Round 1 Start 6 sc in a magic ring (6)
Round 2 2 sc in each sc (12)
Round 3 in blo, sc around (12)
Round 4 *sc dec, sc in next 4 sc* repeat twice (10)
Round 5 sc around (10)

Change to red yarn
Round 6 *sc dec, sc in next 3 sc* repeat twice (8)
Round 7 sc around (8)
sl st in next sc and tie off, leave long tail
Stuff firmly
Make 2

TO ASSEMBLE BABYBOT

- Embroider the face and the embellishments before assembling the head. The eyebrows are made using the metallic gray floss, and formed using two French knots each. Check the photograph on the preceding page to place them correctly.
- Using a double strand of black floss, start by stitching squares for the eyes, referring to the photograph to place them on the face. They are made from long, overlapping single stitches, placed horizontally and arranged one above the other to make a solid square. The mouth is made in the same way, but in the shape of a long, narrow rectangle.
- The eyelashes are made with single stitches. Position them carefully.
- When all the features are in place, sew up the pieces to form the head. Leave a small gap for filling, then pack firmly with tiny pieces of toy stuffing. Stitch up the gap using the yarn needle, and squeeze the head into a neat, square shape.
- Sew on the combination receivers/ears, using the tails of yarn left from the crocheting.
- Cut a tiny square of white felt for the front panel. Make the controls with two chain stitches and two French knots in metallic floss. Then stitch it onto the front of the body using white sewing thread and a tiny overstitch around the edges.
- Stuff the body and sew the head onto it using the tail of yarn left from the crocheting.
- Finally, stuff and sew on Babybot's arms and legs.

BLUEPRINT

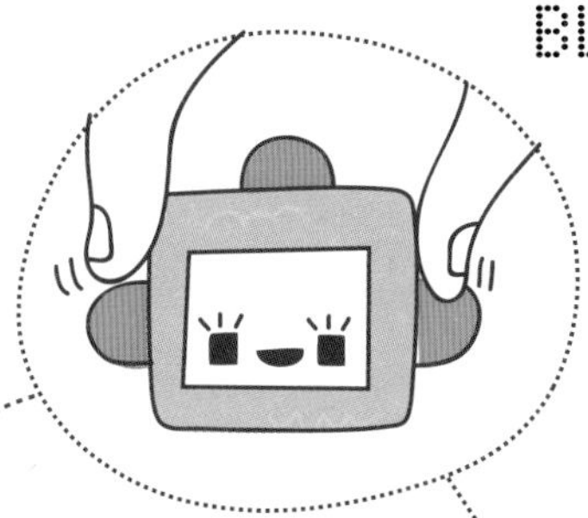

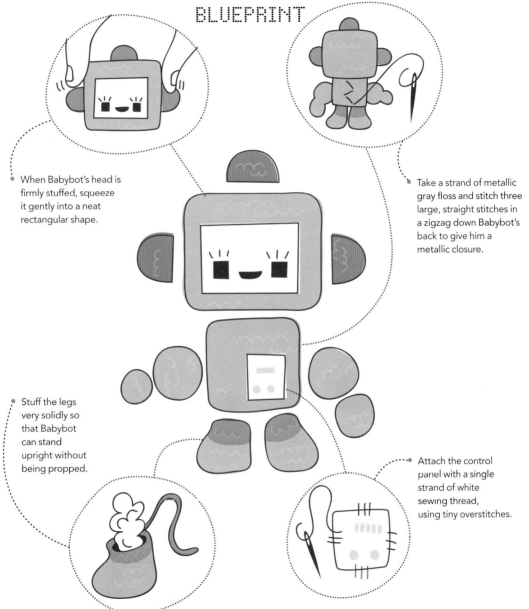

When Babybot's head is firmly stuffed, squeeze it gently into a neat rectangular shape.

Take a strand of metallic gray floss and stitch three large, straight stitches in a zigzag down Babybot's back to give him a metallic closure.

Stuff the legs very solidly so that Babybot can stand upright without being propped.

Attach the control panel with a single strand of white sewing thread, using tiny overstitches.

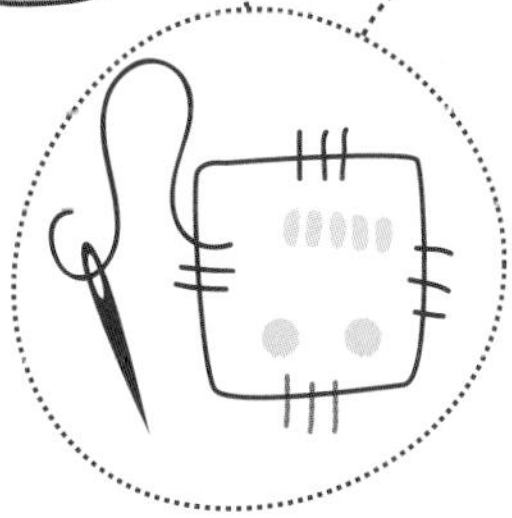

COSMIC BEAR

If it's written in the stars, Cosmic Bear will be able to work it out for you. Were it not for the strongly stitched rivet that bolts the two sides of his head together, you might mistake him for a regular teddy, but he's much more hardworking. The levers in his stomach allow you to compute his astral predictions, and his gaze is cast slightly skyward for some practical stargazing.

YOU WILL NEED

- crochet hook, size C2 (2.75 mm)
- stitch marker or paper clip
- 1 yarn needle
- 1 embroidery needle
- 1 beading needle
- toy stuffing to stuff the bot
- blue yarn
- black yarn (for the mouth)
- black embroidery floss (2 strands)
- white embroidery floss (1 strand)
- blue embroidery floss (1 strand)
- metallic thread
- 3 silver bugle beads, ¼ inch (7 mm) long
- 2 black beads, ⅛ inch (4 mm) in diameter
- small scrap of white felt for the eyes and nose
- glue stick
- small white beads

SKILL LEVEL

✱✱

TO MAKE COSMIC BEAR

To make the head, using blue yarn

Round 1 Start 6 sc in a magic ring (6)
Round 2 2 sc in each sc around (12)
Round 3 *2 sc in next sc, sc in next sc* repeat 6 times (18)
Round 4 *2 sc in next sc, sc in next 2 sc* repeat 6 times (24)
Round 5 *2 sc in next sc, sc in next 3 sc* repeat 6 times (30)
Rounds 6 to 10 sc in each sc around (30)
Round 11 *sc dec, sc in next 3 sc* repeat 6 times (24)
Round 12 *sc dec, sc in next 2 sc* repeat 6 times (18)
Stuff firmly
sl st in next sc and tie off, weave in the end yarn

To make the body, using blue yarn

Round 1 Start 6 sc in a magic ring (6)
Round 2 2 sc in each sc around (12)
Round 3 *2 sc in next sc, 1 sc in next sc* repeat 6 times (18)
Rounds 4 to 7 sc in each sc around (18)
Round 8 *sc in next sc, sc dec* repeat 6 times (12)
Round 9 sc in each sc around (12)
Stuff firmly
sl st in next sc and tie off, leave long tail to attach to head

ABBREVIATIONS: **ch** = *chain* **st** = *stitch* **sl st** = *slip stitch* **sc** = *single crochet* **hdc** = *half-double crochet* **sc dec** = *single crochet decrease (decrease over 2 stitches)* **blo** = *back loops only* * = *repeat instructions between asterisks*

To make the arms, using blue yarn
Round 1 Start 4 sc in a magic ring (4)
Round 2 *sc in next sc, 2 sc in next sc* repeat twice (6)
Rounds 3 to 4 sc in each sc around (6)
Stuff a little
sl st in next sc and tie off, leave long tail to attach to body
Make 2

To make the legs, using blue yarn
Round 1 Start 4 sc in a magic ring (4)
Round 2 2 sc in each sc around (8)
Rounds 3 to 4 sc in each sc around (8)
Stuff a little
sl st in next sc and tie off, leave long tail to attach to body
Make 2

To make the ears, using blue yarn
ch 4, *sc, hdc* in 2nd ch from hook, 3 dc in next st, *hdc, sc* in last ch
Tie off, leave long tail to attach to head
Make 2

TO ASSEMBLE COSMIC BEAR

- Stuff the head firmly. Using the metallic thread, chain stitch a line around the center of the head, from the base of the back of the head to the base of the front.
- Cut a tiny circle of white felt for the nose and embroider a small black inverted triangle in the center of it, using two strands of black floss and straight stitches. Use a single strand of white floss and tiny overstitching to attach Cosmic Bear's nose to his face.
- For the eyes, cut two tiny ovals of white felt, glue them in position on Cosmic Bear's face, then sew on two black beads for the pupils. Embroider the mouth in a straight single stitch, using black yarn. Sew some little white beads on either side of Cosmic Bear's head rivet, using a single strand of white floss and the beading needle.
- Pin the ears into place and sew them onto the head with leftover tails of yarn.
- Stuff Cosmic Bear's body firmly and sew the levers to his front using metallic thread. Make the three vertical lines with chain stitch, then add three bugle beads for the levers, stitching them across the lines at three different levels with a beading needle and one strand of blue floss.
- Stuff the legs and sew them onto the body using tails of yarn left from crocheting. Sew Cosmic Bear's head onto his body, and complete him by sewing his arms in place at his sides.

BLUEPRINT

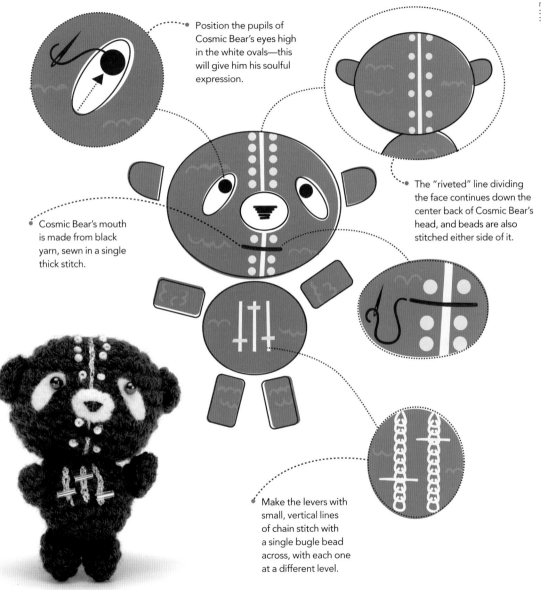

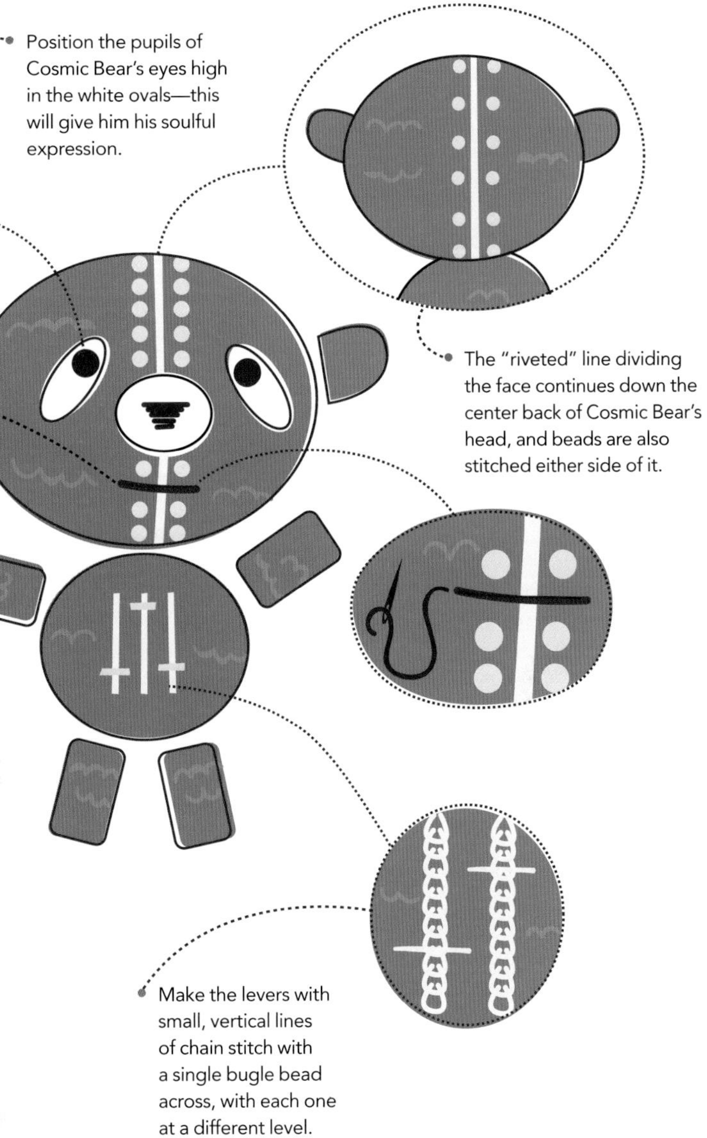
Position the pupils of Cosmic Bear's eyes high in the white ovals—this will give him his soulful expression.
The "riveted" line dividing the face continues down the center back of Cosmic Bear's head, and beads are also stitched either side of it.
Cosmic Bear's mouth is made from black yarn, sewn in a single thick stitch.
Make the levers with small, vertical lines of chain stitch with a single bugle bead across, with each one at a different level.

THINKER

There's nothing anthropomorphic about Thinker—he's all bot. His pure white body and decorative finishing touches give him a fresh, pristine look, and his large head and spindly embroidered arms offer a hint that this crobot's skill lies mainly in his analytic abilities. With his sweetly wistful face, he makes a peaceful desktop friend.

YOU WILL NEED

- crochet hook, size C2 (2.75 mm)
- stitch marker or paper clip
- 1 yarn needle
- 1 embroidery needle
- 1 beading needle
- toy stuffing to stuff the bot
- white yarn
- burgundy yarn
- black embroidery floss (2 strands)
- burgundy embroidery floss (1 strand)
- 6 burgundy beads, ⅛ inch (4 mm) in diameter
- 4 sequins—2 blue, 2 silver
- 4 tiny clear beads

SKILL LEVEL

TO MAKE THINKER

To make the head, using white yarn

Round 1 Start 6 sc in a magic ring (6)
Round 2 2 sc in each sc around (12)
Round 3 *2 sc in next sc, sc in next sc* repeat 6 times (18)
Round 4 *2 sc in next sc, sc in next 2 sc* repeat 6 times (24)
Round 5 *2 sc in next sc, sc in next 3 sc* repeat 6 times (30)
Rounds 6 to 10 sc in each sc around (30)
Round 11 *sc dec, sc in next 3 sc* repeat 6 times (24)
Round 12 *sc dec, sc in next 2 sc* repeat 6 times (18)
Round 13 *sc dec, sc in next sc* repeat 6 times (12)
Stuff firmly
sl st in next sc and tie off, weave in the end yarn

To make the body, using white yarn

Round 1 Start 6 sc in a magic ring (6)
Round 2 2 sc in each sc around (12)
Round 3 *2 sc in next sc, sc in next sc* repeat 6 times (18)
Round 4 *2 sc in next sc, sc in next 2 sc* repeat 6 times (24)
Round 5 in blo *sc in each sc around* (24)
Rounds 6 to 10 sc in each sc around (24)
Round 11 *sc dec, sc in next 2 sc* repeat 6 times (18)
Stuff firmly
sl st in next sc and tie off, leave long tail to sew to head

To make the ears, using burgundy yarn

Round 1 Start 6 sc in a magic ring (6)
Round 2 2 sc in each sc around (12)

ABBREVIATIONS: **ch** = *chain* **st** = *stitch* **sl st** = *slip stitch* **sc** = *single crochet* **hdc** = *half-double crochet* **sc dec** = *single crochet decrease (decrease over 2 stitches)* **blo** = *back loops only* * = *repeat instructions between asterisks*

Round 3 in blo *sc dec, sc in next 4 sc* repeat twice (10)
Round 4 sc in each sc around (10)
sl st in next sc and tie off, leaving long tail to sew to head
Stuff firmly
Make 2

TO ASSEMBLE THINKER

- Stuff the head firmly and stitch it closed.
- Embroider the face details. The eyes are made using two strands of black floss and straight stitches, gradually reducing in length from the base to make a triangular shape. Thinker's mouth is made from a line of short, straight stitches aligned with the bottom of his eyes. Check the photograph to make sure you have the placement right.
- Stuff the ears so that they are slightly padded. Add the sequins—a different color for each ear—by sewing them on with a single strand of burgundy floss and stitching a clear bead into the center of each. Sew the ears onto the head with leftover tails of yarn.
- Stuff the body firmly. Embroider the arms and fingers with two strands of black floss, using lines of long backstitch. Attach beads at the end of each finger with one strand of burgundy floss. Alternatively, you could embroider little French knots for the fingers, in which case use the full thickness of burgundy embroidery floss (6 strands).
- Pin Thinker's head into place and attach it to his body with a leftover tail of yarn.

BLUEPRINT

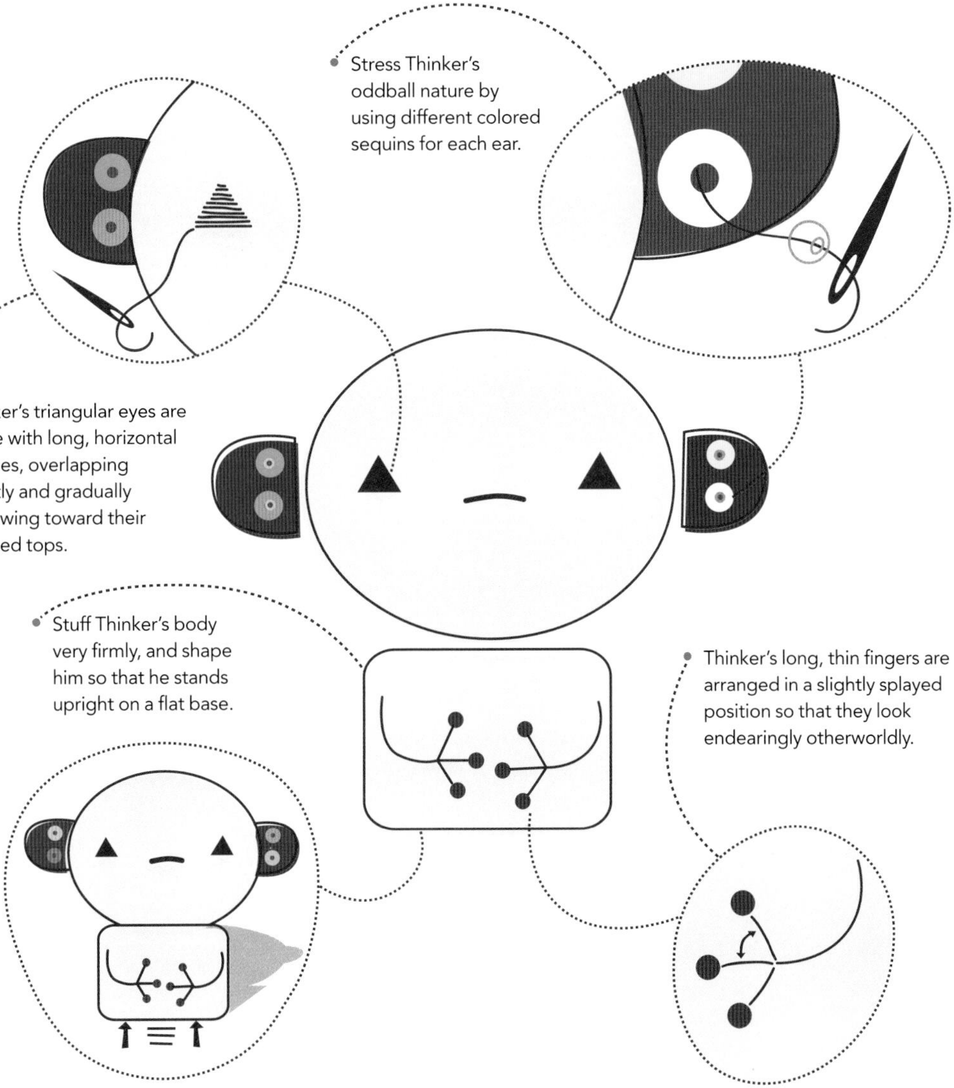

Stress Thinker's oddball nature by using different colored sequins for each ear.

Thinker's triangular eyes are made with long, horizontal stitches, overlapping slightly and gradually narrowing toward their pointed tops.

Stuff Thinker's body very firmly, and shape him so that he stands upright on a flat base.

Thinker's long, thin fingers are arranged in a slightly splayed position so that they look endearingly otherworldly.

WHEELY

Wheely has no need for arms or legs—she has a pair of wheels to roll her out and about! She has a pleasant but minimal face, a rounded body, and a tiny, touching heart embroidered with minute red beads. Although she isn't as complicated as some of her crobot friends, her finishing and details must be immaculately executed to give her a characteristically clean and tidy appearance.

YOU WILL NEED

- crochet hook, size C2 (2.75 mm)
- stitch marker or paper clip
- 1 yarn needle
- 1 embroidery needle
- 1 beading needle
- toy stuffing to stuff the bot
- yellow yarn
- black yarn
- black embroidery floss (2 strands)
- red embroidery floss (2 strands)
- gray embroidery floss (2 strands)
- 2 black bugle beads, ¼ inch (7 mm) long
- 8 small red beads
- scraps of red and blue felt (for the front buttons)
- 1 screw, ½ inch (12 mm) long

SKILL LEVEL

✱✱

TO MAKE WHEELY

To make the head, using yellow yarn

Round 1 Start 6 sc in a magic ring (6)
Don't pull the tail of your magic ring too tightly, as you will need to pass a screw through the center hole
Round 2 2 sc in each sc around (12)
Round 3 *2 sc in next sc, sc in next sc* repeat 6 times (18)
Round 4 *2 sc in next sc, sc in next 2 sc* repeat 6 times (24)
Rounds 5 to 12 sc in each sc around (24)
sl st in next sc and tie off, weave in the end yarn
Stuff firmly

To make the body, using yellow yarn

Round 1 Start 6 sc in a magic ring (6)
Round 2 2 sc in each sc around (12)
Round 3 *2 sc in next sc, sc in next sc* repeat 6 times (18)
Round 4 *2 sc in next sc, sc in next 2 sc* repeat 6 times (24)
Round 5 *2 sc in next sc, sc in next 3 sc* repeat 6 times (30)
Round 6 in blo sc in each sc around (30)
Round 7 *sc dec, sc in next 3 sc* repeat 6 times (24)
Stuff firmly
sl st in next sc and tie off, leave long tail to sew to head

ABBREVIATIONS: ch = *chain* **st** = *stitch* **sl st** = *slip stitch* **sc** = *single crochet* **hdc** = *half-double crochet* **sc dec** = *single crochet decrease (decrease over 2 stitches)* **blo** = *back loops only* * = *repeat instructions between asterisks*

To make the wheels, using black yarn
Round 1 Start 6 sc in a magic ring (6)
Round 2 2 sc in each sc (12)
Round 3 *2 sc in next sc, sc in next sc* repeat 6 times (18)
Rounds 4 to 5 sc in each sc around (18)
Round 6 *sc dec, sc in next sc* repeat 6 times (12)
Round 7 sc dec around (6)
sl st in next sc and tie off, leave long tail to sew to body
Flatten the piece
Make 2

TO ASSEMBLE WHEELY

- Use a single strand of black floss and a beading needle to sew on the bugle beads for Wheely's eyes. Place them carefully, looking at the position in the photograph. Use the same thread to embroider a little mouth between the eyes with a single, horizontal straight stitch.
- Attach the head to the body with the tail of yarn left from crocheting, and stuff Wheely firmly before closing her up. Cut two pieces of felt, one red, one blue. Attach these to the body using two strands of black floss and crossing the thread over the top of the felt pieces, using the picture for reference.
- Using the beading needle threaded with two strands of red floss, embroider a little heart on Wheely's front, placing beads around the edges and in the center as shown in the photograph.
- Use the embroidery needle and two strands of red thread to sew the central line around Wheely's body. You can use small overlapping straight stitches or a chain stitch for this.
- Flatten out the wheels with your finger. Using two strands of gray embroidery floss, chain stitch the details onto the wheels—each has a small central circle and six straight spokes. Then attach the wheels to the body using leftover tails of yarn.
- Attach the screw to Wheely by gently pushing it about halfway into the center top of her head.

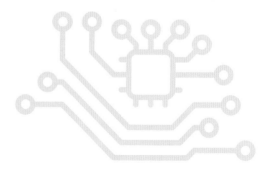

BLUEPRINT

Gently work the screw about halfway into the top of Wheely's head; it should be deep enough to stay securely in place.

The wheel centers and spokes are embroidered with chain stitch, using two strands of gray floss.

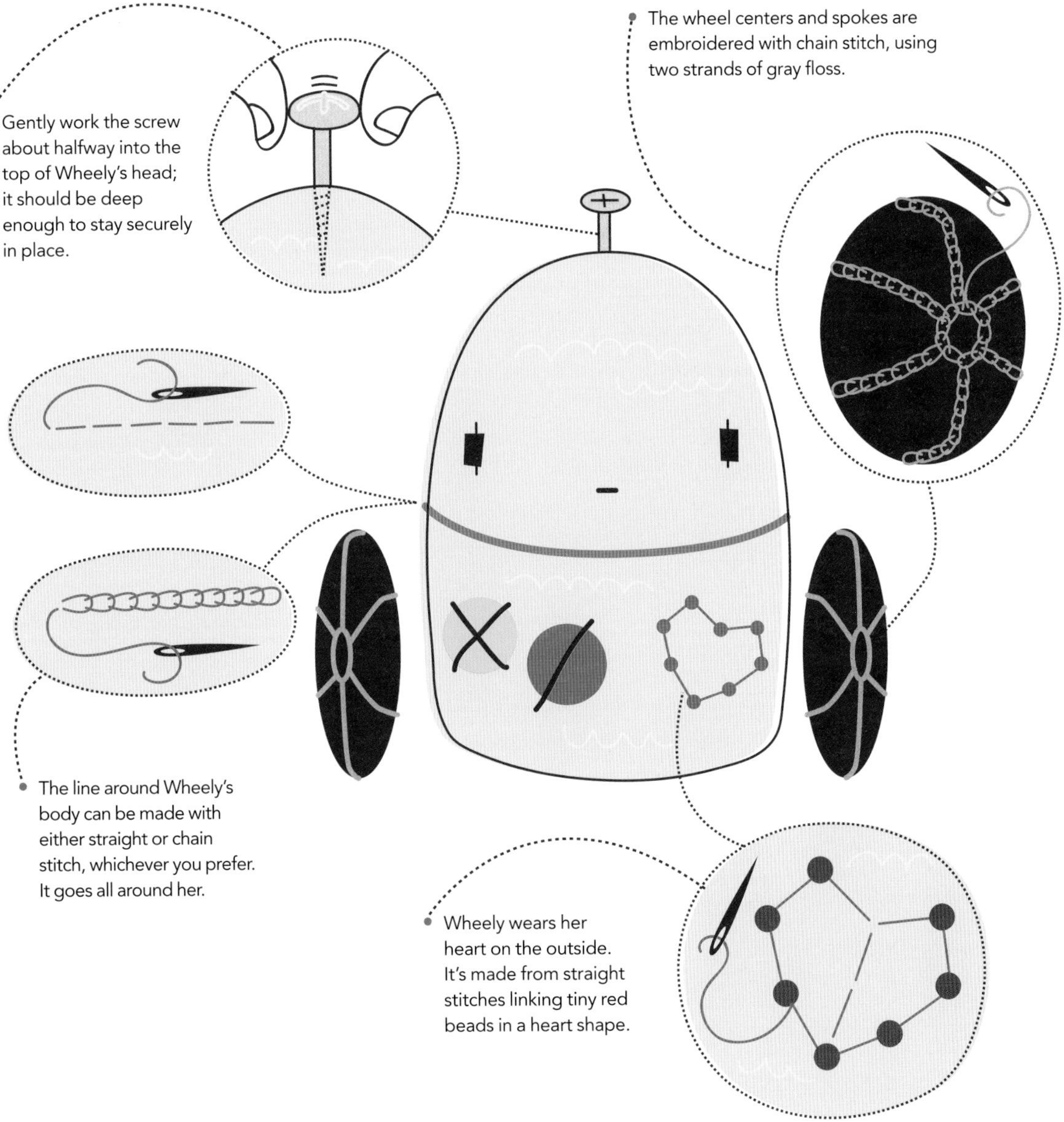

The line around Wheely's body can be made with either straight or chain stitch, whichever you prefer. It goes all around her.

Wheely wears her heart on the outside. It's made from straight stitches linking tiny red beads in a heart shape.

SPACE MOUSE

Space Mouse has a slightly pointed head, big satellite-dish ears, and a lavishly curly tail. Exposed wiring around her legs and the edges of her ears reveals her robotic status, and her keen black eyes can see a long way. Little ricrac and snap fastener details make up her unusual control panel, and her large, vertical eyes lend her an alert, ready-to-go look.

YOU WILL NEED

- crochet hook, size C2 (2.75 mm)
- stitch marker or paper clip
- 1 yarn needle
- 1 embroidery needle
- 1 beading needle
- toy stuffing to stuff the bot
- purple yarn
- black yarn
- metallic sewing thread
- metallic gray embroidery floss (1 strand)
- white embroidery floss (1 strand)
- 2 small silver snap fasteners
- 1 star-shaped silver sequin
- 1 tiny clear bead
- scrap of white ricrac braid

SKILL LEVEL

TO MAKE SPACE MOUSE

To make the head, using purple yarn

Round 1 Start 6 sc in a magic ring (6)
Round 2 2 sc in each sc around (12)
Round 3 *2 sc in next sc, sc in next 3 sc* repeat 3 times (15)
Round 4 sc in each sc around (15)
Round 5 *2 sc in next sc, sc in next 4 sc* repeat 3 times (18)
Round 6 *2 sc in next sc, sc in next 2 sc* repeat 6 times (24)
Round 7 *2 sc in next sc, sc in next 3 sc* repeat 6 times (30)
Rounds 8 to 11 sc in each sc around (30)
Round 12 *sc dec, sc in next 3 sc* repeat 6 times (24)
Round 13 *sc dec, sc in next 2 sc* repeat 6 times (18)
Round 14 *sc dec, sc in next sc* repeat 6 times (12)
Stuff firmly
sl st in next sc and tie off, leave long tail to sew to body

To make the ears, using purple yarn

Round 1 Start 6 sc in a magic ring (6)
Round 2 sc in each sc around (12)
Round 3 *2 sc in next sc, sc in next sc* repeat 6 times (18)
Round 4 *2 sc in next sc, sc in next 2 sc* repeat 6 times (24)
sl st in next sc and tie off, leave long tail to sew to head
Make 2

ABBREVIATIONS: ch = *chain* **st** = *stitch* **sl st** = *slip stitch* **sc** = *single crochet* **hdc** = *half-double crochet* **sc dec** = *single crochet decrease (decrease over 2 stitches)* **blo** = *back loops only* ***** = *repeat instructions between asterisks*

To make the legs, using purple yarn
Round 1 Start 4 sc in a magic ring (4)
Round 2 *2 sc in next sc, sc in next sc* repeat twice (6)
Rounds 3 to 8 sc in each sc around (6)
sl st in next sc and tie off, leave long tail to sew to body
Stuff firmly
Make 2

To make the arms, using purple yarn
Round 1 Start 4 sc in a magic ring (4)
Round 2 *2 sc in next sc, sc in next sc* repeat twice (6)
Rounds 3 to 7 sc in each sc around (6)
sl st in next sc and tie off, leave long tail to sew to body
Stuff the hand just a little so that the rest of the arm stays flexible
Make 2

To make the tail, using purple yarn
ch 37 tie off, leave long tail to sew to body

To make the body, using purple yarn
Round 1 Start 6 sc in a magic ring (6)
Round 2 2 sc in each sc around (12)
Round 3 *2 sc in next sc, sc in next 3 sc* repeat 3 times (15)
Rounds 4 to 10 sc in each sc around (15)
Round 11 *sc dec, sc in next 3 sc* repeat 3 times (12)
sl st in next sc and tie off
Stuff firmly

TO ASSEMBLE SPACE MOUSE

- Use the metallic gray floss to make neat overstitches around the edges of both of Space Mouse's ears. Pin the ears in place on the head and sew them on with leftover tails of yarn.
- Thread a yarn needle with black yarn and make Space Mouse's nose and eyes. Each of the eyes is one long, straight stitch; the nose is an inverted triangle of small horizontal stitches. Using backstitch, embroider the line down from the nose with a single strand of black floss.
- Stuff the body and sew on Space Mouse's controls with the metallic gray floss. Secure the braid first, using small stitches down the middle. Use the beading needle to attach the sequin and secure it with a bead in the center at the lower end of the ricrac braid. Add the snap fasteners, using only the lower half of each one.
- Attach the body to the head with the leftover tail of yarn.
- Stuff the legs. Wind a length of metallic gray floss around each leg, stitching it through the bottom, then winding it in five spirals around the leg before stitching through the leg and tying the thread off. Sew the legs to the body with the leftover tails of yarn.
- Attach the arms to the body with the leftover tails of yarn. Bend the folded arm into position and fasten it into place at Space Mouse's side with a single stitch.
- Shape Space Mouse's head to a slight point at the top.
- Attach the tail to Space Mouse's lower back.

BLUEPRINT

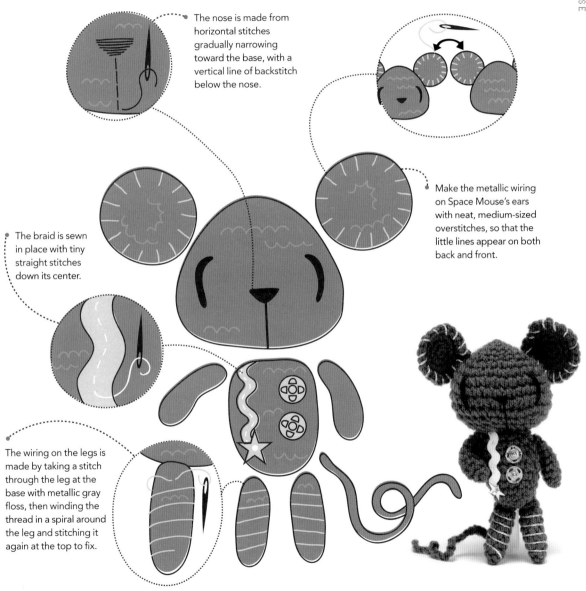

The nose is made from horizontal stitches gradually narrowing toward the base, with a vertical line of backstitch below the nose.

Make the metallic wiring on Space Mouse's ears with neat, medium-sized overstitches, so that the little lines appear on both back and front.

The braid is sewn in place with tiny straight stitches down its center.

The wiring on the legs is made by taking a stitch through the leg at the base with metallic gray floss, then winding the thread in a spiral around the leg and stitching it again at the top to fix.

ALIENBOT

You can tell that this small crobot isn't from any nearby planet. Not only are those big, pointy ears a giveaway but—almost unheard of for a bot—her control panel runs across the top of her head. And her surprised—and slightly apprehensive—face lets you know that she wasn't expecting to find herself in her current surroundings, either. Maybe the best thing you can do is to make her a matching friend (in a contrasting color?) so that they can share their alien experiences.

YOU WILL NEED

- crochet hook, size C2 (2.75 mm)
- stitch marker or paper clip
- 1 yarn needle
- 1 embroidery needle
- 1 beading needle
- toy stuffing to stuff the bot
- pink yarn
- black yarn
- scrap of white felt (for the eyes)
- scrap piece of red felt (for the control panel)
- assortment of multicolored bugle beads, ¼ inch (7 mm) long
- 2 black beads, ⅛ inch (4 mm) in diameter
- 1 metallic bead, ⅛ inch (4 mm) in diameter
- red embroidery floss (1 strand)
- white embroidery floss (1 strand)
- metallic purple thread

SKILL LEVEL

TO MAKE ALIENBOT

To make the head, using pink yarn

Round 1 Start 6 sc in a magic ring (6)
Round 2 2 sc in each sc around (12)
Round 3 *2 sc in next sc, sc in next sc* repeat 6 times (18)
Round 4 *2 sc in next sc, sc in next 2 sc* repeat 6 times (24)
Round 5 *2 sc in next sc, sc in next 3 sc* repeat 6 times (30)
Rounds 6 to 10 sc in each sc around (30)
Round 11 *sc dec, sc in next 3 sc* repeat 6 times (24)
Round 12 *sc dec, sc in next 2 sc* repeat 6 times (18)
Round 13 *sc in next sc, sc dec* repeat 6 times (12)
Stuff firmly
sl st in next sc and tie off, leave long tail to attach to body

To make the body, using pink yarn

Round 1 Start 6 sc in a magic ring (6)
Round 2 2 sc in each sc around (12)
Round 3 *2 sc in next sc, 1 sc in next sc* repeat 6 times (18)

ABBREVIATIONS: **ch** = *chain* **st** = *stitch* **sl st** = *slip stitch* **sc** = *single crochet* **hdc** = *half-double crochet* **sc dec** = *single crochet decrease (decrease over 2 stitches)* **blo** = *back loops only* ***** = *repeat instructions between asterisks*

Round 4 in blo *sc in each sc around* (18)
Rounds 5 to 8 sc in each sc around (18)
Round 9 *sc in next sc, sc dec* repeat 6 times (12)
Stuff firmly
sl st in next sc and tie off, weave in the end yarn

To make the arms, using pink yarn

Round 1 Start 4 sc in a magic ring (4)
Round 2 *sc in next sc, 2 sc in next sc* repeat twice (6)
Rounds 3 to 4 sc in each sc around (6)
Stuff a little
sl st in next sc and tie off, leave long tail to attach to body
Make 2

To make the legs, using pink yarn

Round 1 Start 4 sc in a magic ring (4)
Round 2 *sc in next sc, 2 sc in next sc* repeat twice (6)
Round 3 sc in each sc around (6)
Stuff a little
sl st in next sc and tie off, leave long tail to attach to body
Make 2

To make the eyes, using black yarn

Round 1 Start 6 sc in a magic ring (6)
Round 2 2 sc in each sc around (12)
sl st in next sc and tie off, leave long tail to sew to head
Make 2

To make the ears, using pink yarn

Round 1 Start 4 sc in a magic ring (4)
Round 2 *2 sc in next sc, sc in next sc* repeat twice (6)
Round 3 *2 sc in next sc, sc in next 2 sc* repeat twice (8)
Rounds 4 to 7 sc in each sc around (8)
Round 8 *sc dec, sc in next 2 sc* repeat twice (6)
sl st in next sc and tie off, leave long tail to attach to head
Make 2

TO ASSEMBLE ALIENBOT

- Make the eyes from two small, round pieces of white felt, a little smaller than the black crocheted eye circles. Using a beading needle and a single strand of black floss, sew a black bead onto each of the felt circles, experimenting with positioning to give Alienbot her slightly apprehensive expression. Stitch the pieces of felt to the black eye circles using a small overstitch with one strand of white floss.
- Stuff the head firmly. Then sew on the eyes using the black tails of yarn left over from the crocheting.
- Cut a small, long rectangle of red felt, trying it against Alienbot's head for size. It should come down to the tops of her eyes at the front, and to about the same point on the back of her head. Thread a beading needle with one strand of red floss and sew multicolored bugle beads along it, alternating the colors. Then stitch it in position on the head, using tiny overstitches.
- Flatten the ears a little, then pin them in place and sew them onto the head with the tails of yarn left over from crocheting.
- Stuff the body firmly. Using the metallic purple thread, chain stitch a little arch in the middle of the body, and add a metallic bead just underneath it.
- Sew the head to the body using the tail of yarn left over from crocheting.
- Lightly stuff the arms and legs and attach them to the body with the tails of yarn left from crocheting.

BLUEPRINT

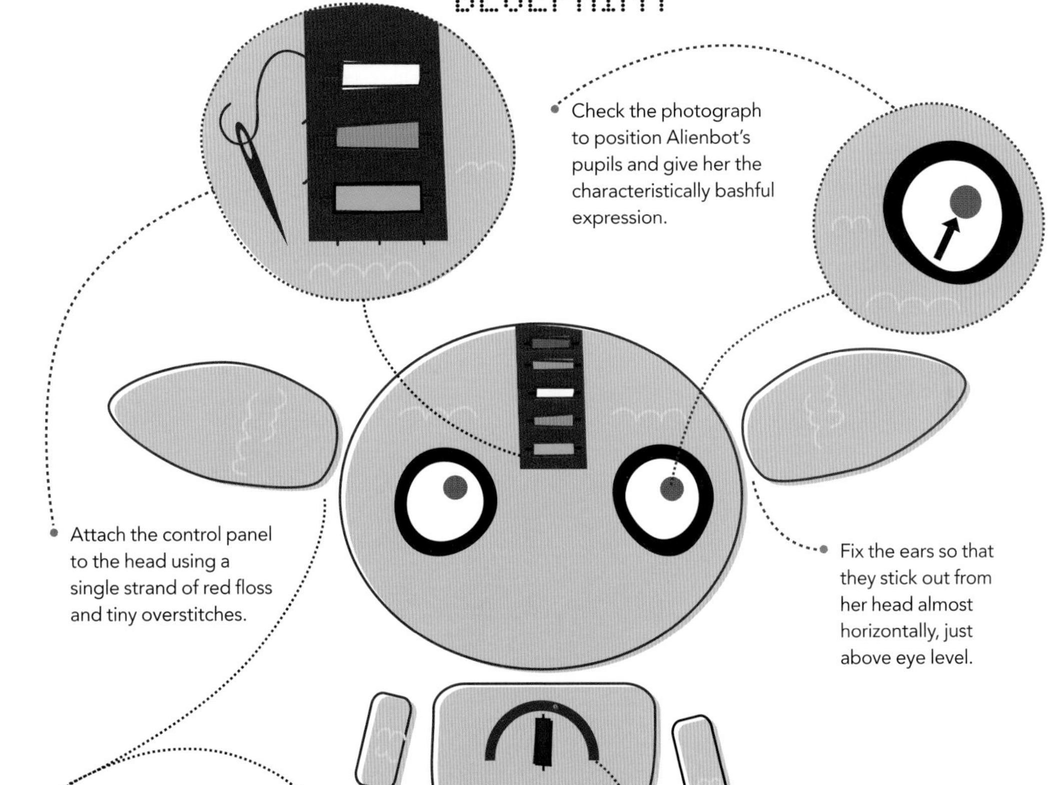

Check the photograph to position Alienbot's pupils and give her the characteristically bashful expression.

Attach the control panel to the head using a single strand of red floss and tiny overstitches.

Fix the ears so that they stick out from her head almost horizontally, just above eye level.

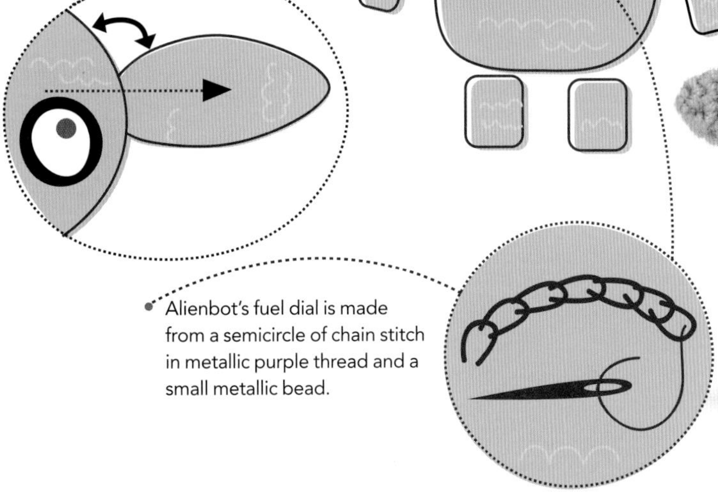

Alienbot's fuel dial is made from a semicircle of chain stitch in metallic purple thread and a small metallic bead.

BOUNCEBOT

Round and energetic, Bouncebot has gleaming, multifaceted eyes, a rich assortment of controls, and a rolling, bouncy walk. Despite his slightly blank expression, he radiates a cheerful, positive air—use him to brighten up the "To Do" pile on your desk, or sit him on a corner of the kitchen counter so that he can keep an eye on who is coming and going around the house.

YOU WILL NEED

- crochet hook, size C2 (2.5 mm)
- stitch marker or paper clip
- 1 yarn needle
- 1 embroidery needle
- 1 beading needle
- toy stuffing to stuff the bot
- blue yarn
- yellow yarn
- black yarn
- scrap of white felt
- 6 red bugle beads, ¼ inch (7 mm) long
- 1 green sequin and 1 small green bead to secure it in place
- 5 red sequins
- 8 tiny red beads
- 1 gold bugle bead, ¼ inch (7 mm) long
- 2 flat, black faceted beads, ¼ inch (7 mm) in diameter (for the eyes)
- black embroidery floss
- red embroidery floss
- white embroidery floss
- gray embroidery floss
- 2 pins with black bead heads (available at craft stores; use to finish the arms)
- 2 small faceted nuts, about ½ inch (1 cm) in diameter
- 1 tiny tire valve to make Bouncebot's antenna

SKILL LEVEL

TO MAKE BOUNCEBOT

To make the head, using blue yarn

Round 1 Start 6 sc in a magic ring (6)
Round 2 2 sc in each sc around (12)
Round 3 *2 sc in next sc, sc in next sc* repeat 6 times (18)
Round 4 *2 sc in next sc, sc in next 2 sc* repeat 6 times (24)
Rounds 5 to 9 sc in each sc around (24)
Round 10 *sc dec, sc in next 2 sc* repeat 6 times (18)
Round 11 *sc in next sc, sc dec* repeat 6 times (12)
Stuff firmly
Round 12 sc dec around (6)
sl st in next sc and tie off, leave a long tail to attach to body

To make the body, using yellow and blue yarn

Start with yellow yarn
Round 1 Start 6 sc in a magic ring (6)

ABBREVIATIONS: **ch** = *chain* **st** = *stitch* **sl st** = *slip stitch* **sc** = *single crochet* **hdc** = *half-double crochet* **sc dec** = *single crochet decrease (decrease over 2 stitches)* **blo** = *back loops only* * = *repeat instructions between asterisks*

Round 2 2 sc in each sc around (12)
Round 3 *2 sc in next sc, sc in next sc* repeat 6 times (18)
Round 4 *2 sc in next sc, sc in next 2 sc* repeat 6 times (24)
Round 5 *2 sc in next sc, sc in next 3 sc* repeat 6 times (30)
Rounds 6 to 8 sc in each sc around (30)

Change to blue yarn
Rounds 9 to 10 sc in each sc around (30)
Round 11 *sc dec, sc in next 3 sc* repeat 6 times (24)
Round 12 *sc dec, sc in next 2 sc* repeat 6 times (18)
Round 13 *sc in next sc, sc dec* repeat 6 times (12)
Stuff firmly
Round 14 sc dec around (6)
sl st in next sc and tie off, weave in the end yarn

To make the base, using black yarn
Round 1 Start 6 sc in a magic ring (6)
Round 2 2 sc in each sc around (12)
Round 3 *2 sc in next sc, sc in next sc* repeat 6 times (18)
Round 4 *2 sc in next sc, sc in next 2 sc* repeat 6 times (24)
Round 5 *2 sc in next sc, sc in next 3 sc* repeat 6 times (30)
Round 6 *2 sc in next sc, sc in next 4 sc* repeat 6 times (36)
sl st in next sc and tie off, leave long tail to attach to body

TO ASSEMBLE BOUNCEBOT

- Stuff the head firmly. Cut a small rectangle of white felt for the eye panel, referring to the photograph and trying it against the head to ensure it is the right size. When it fits, round off the corners with a pair of scissors. Stitch the eye panel onto the head using a single strand of white floss and tiny overstitches. Rethread the needle with two strands of black floss, and backstitch a line down the center of the felt to separate the eye spaces.
- Thread a beading needle with one strand of blue floss, and sew a row of five small sequins along Bouncebot's forehead. First thread a sequin onto the thread, then one of the tiny red beads. Thread the needle back through the central hole of the sequin, then back onto Bouncebot's head, and repeat with the other four sequins and beads. Use the same thread to sew a gold bugle bead for the mouth; to get the slightly quizzical expression, sew it on a little crooked. Stitch the valve firmly to the top of Bouncebot's head, using one strand of blue floss.
- Cut a triangle from the white felt, trying it against Bouncebot's body for size. Using a beading needle and one strand of red floss, sew on the row of red beads and the green sequin, secured in place with the green bead.
- Thread an embroidery needle with one strand of white floss and sew the triangle to the body with tiny overstitches.
- Using the beading needle and one strand of blue floss, sew three bugle beads onto the body, to one side of the triangle, lined up in a horizontal "block." Repeat on the other side.
- Using the embroidery needle threaded with one strand of gray floss, sew the nuts into position for the arms. Overstitch around the edges to secure them. Then place one bead-headed pin in the center of each nut.
- Finally, use the tail of yarn left from the crocheting to sew the black base to the underside of Bouncebot's rounded body.

BLUEPRINT

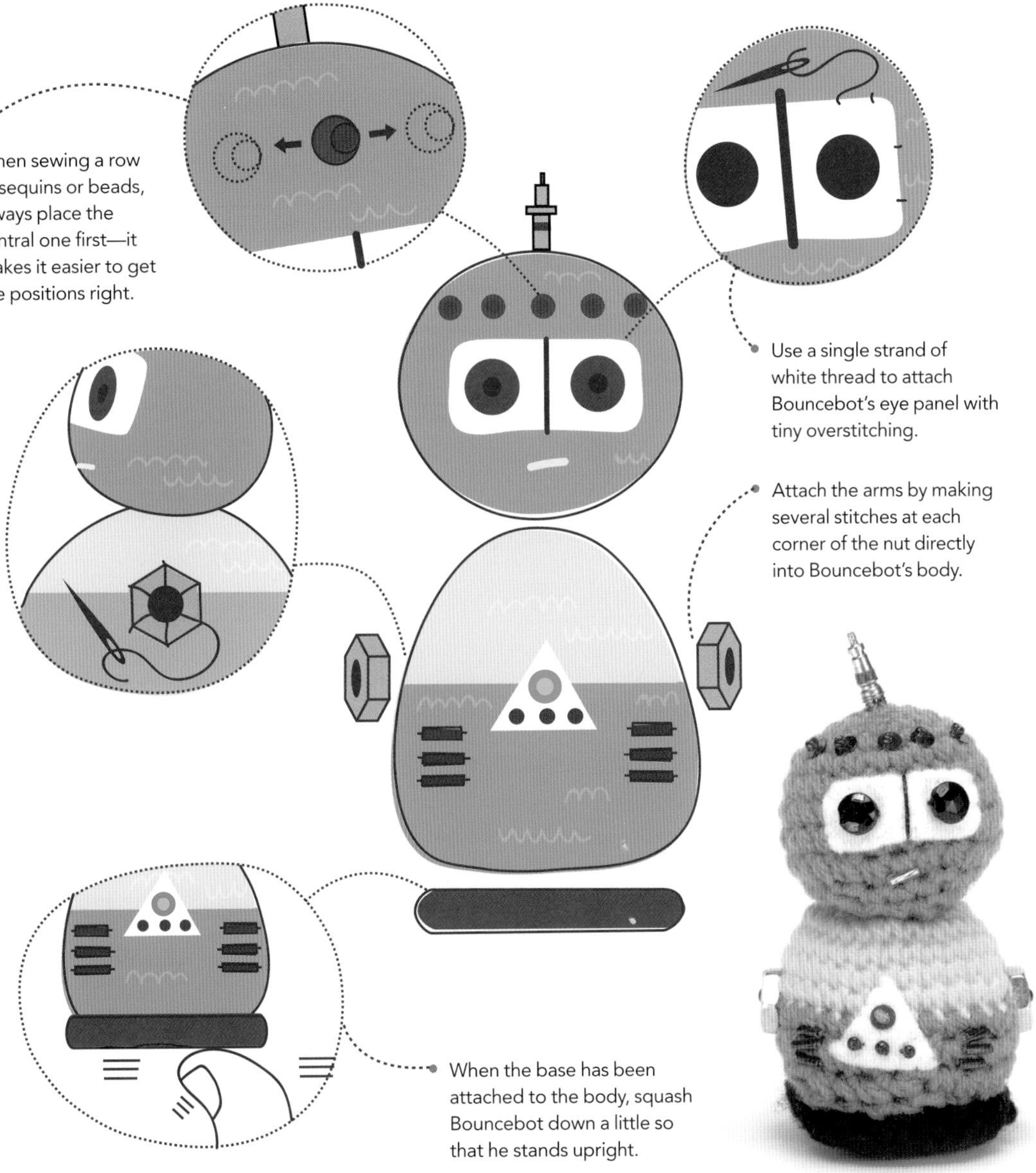

When sewing a row of sequins or beads, always place the central one first—it makes it easier to get the positions right.

Use a single strand of white thread to attach Bouncebot's eye panel with tiny overstitching.

Attach the arms by making several stitches at each corner of the nut directly into Bouncebot's body.

When the base has been attached to the body, squash Bouncebot down a little so that he stands upright.

MATRYOSHKA

Matryoshka is a housekeeping crobot par excellence. Her mother was a babushka and her father was a robot, which takes her skills into a high league of efficiency indeed. Her rivets, dials, and switches show that she's quite technical at heart, but her round, comfortable shape gives her a sturdy, cheerful presence. If you were hard-hearted enough to squeeze her tightly, she'd make an excellent stress ball.

YOU WILL NEED

- crochet hook, size C2 (2.75 mm)
- stitch marker or paper clip
- 1 yarn needle
- 1 embroidery needle
- 1 beading needle
- toy stuffing to stuff the bot
- red yarn
- white yarn
- tiny scrap of white felt
- three green beads, ⅛ inch (4 mm) in diameter
- three gold sequins
- three tiny black beads (to secure sequins in place)
- black embroidery floss (2 strands)
- red embroidery floss (2 strands)
- blue embroidery floss (2 strands)
- white embroidery floss (1 strand)
- 1 tiny tire valve to make Matryoshka's antenna

SKILL LEVEL

✹✹✹

TO MAKE MATRYOSHKA

To make the body, using red yarn

Round 1 Start 6 sc in a magic ring (6)
Round 2 2 sc in each sc around (12)
Round 3 *2 sc in next sc, sc in next sc* repeat 6 times (18)
Round 4 sc in each sc around (18)
Round 5 *2 sc in next sc, sc in next 2 sc* repeat 6 times (24)
Round 6 *2 sc in next sc, sc in next 5 sc* repeat 4 times (28)
Rounds 7 to 10 sc in each sc around (28)
Round 11 *2 sc in next sc, sc in next 13 sc* repeat twice (30)
Rounds 12 to 13 sc in each sc around (30)
Round 14 *sc dec, sc in next 13 sc* repeat twice (28)
Rounds 15 to 16 sc in each sc around (28)
Round 17 *sc dec, sc in next 5 sc* repeat 4 times (24)
Round 18 *sc dec, sc in next 2 sc* repeat 6 times (18)
Round 19 *sc in next sc, sc dec* repeat 6 times (12)
Round 20 sc in each sc around (12)
Stuff firmly
Round 21 sc dec around (6)
sl st in next sc and tie off, leave long tail to close up the hole

ABBREVIATIONS: **ch** = *chain* **st** = *stitch* **sl st** = *slip stitch* **sc** = *single crochet* **hdc** = *half-double crochet* **sc dec** = *single crochet decrease (decrease over 2 stitches)* **blo** = *back loops only* ***** = *repeat instructions between asterisks*

To make the face, using white yarn
Round 1 Start 6 sc in a magic ring (6)
Round 2 2 sc in each sc around (12)
Round 3 *2 sc in next sc, sc in next sc* repeat 6 times (18)
Round 4 *2 sc in next sc, sc in next 2 sc* repeat 6 times (24)
Round 5 *2 sc in next sc, sc in next 3 sc* repeat 3 times (15)
sl st in next sc and tie off, weave in the end yarn

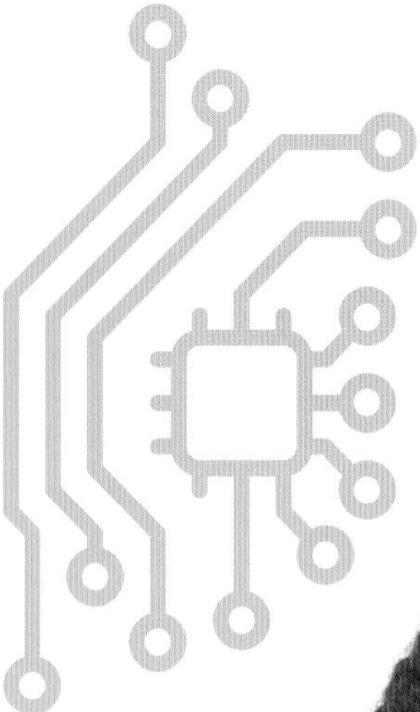

TO ASSEMBLE MATRYOSHKA

- Begin by embroidering the face. Thread an embroidery needle with two strands of black floss and backstitch the zigzag line down the center of the face, following the photograph for positioning. Once you have sewn the main line, create a dotted second line with small running stitches, following the shape of the first. Stitch the eyelids and lashes with single straight stitches, then thread the needle with two strands of blue floss and embroider the irises with several straight, overlapping stitches.
- For the cross-shaped mouth, thread the embroidery needle with two strands of red floss and make two tiny straight stitches, one horizontal and one vertical.
- Thread the needle with one strand of white floss and use small overstitches to attach the face to the body.
- Use the beading needle and one strand of red floss to attach the row of sequins. Thread a sequin and a bead onto the needle and pull the thread back through the center of the sequin to secure it in place on Matryoshka's front. Sew the row of green beads under the sequin "switches."
- Cut two small round pieces of white felt for the dials and overstitch them onto the body with one strand of white floss. Embroider the dial details with two strands each of black thread and red thread, using neat straight stitches.
- Use the beading needle and two strands of red floss to attach the little valve antenna to the top of the head.
- Firmly shape Matryoshka's body into a neat, even oval shape.

BLUEPRINT

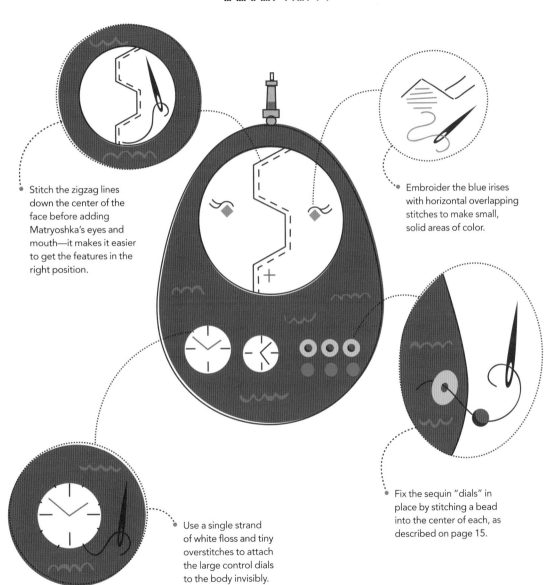

Stitch the zigzag lines down the center of the face before adding Matryoshka's eyes and mouth—it makes it easier to get the features in the right position.

Embroider the blue irises with horizontal overlapping stitches to make small, solid areas of color.

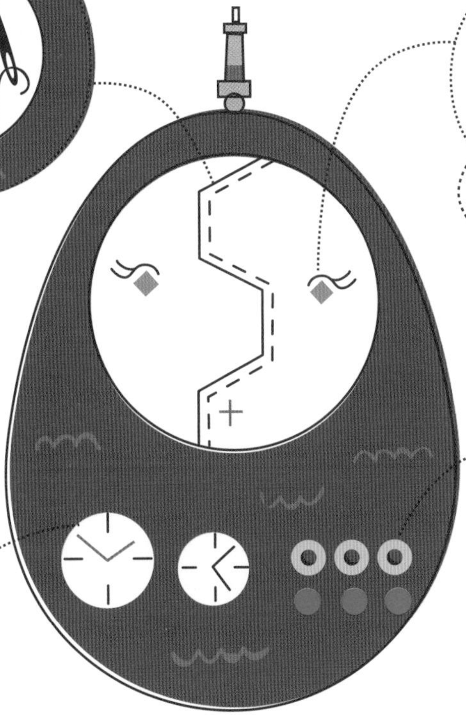

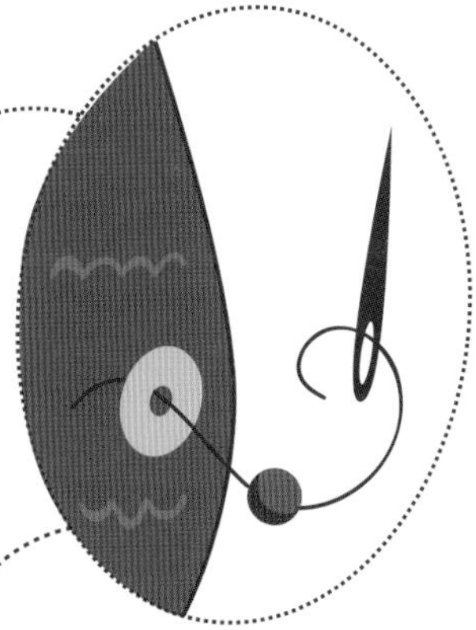

Fix the sequin "dials" in place by stitching a bead into the center of each, as described on page 15.

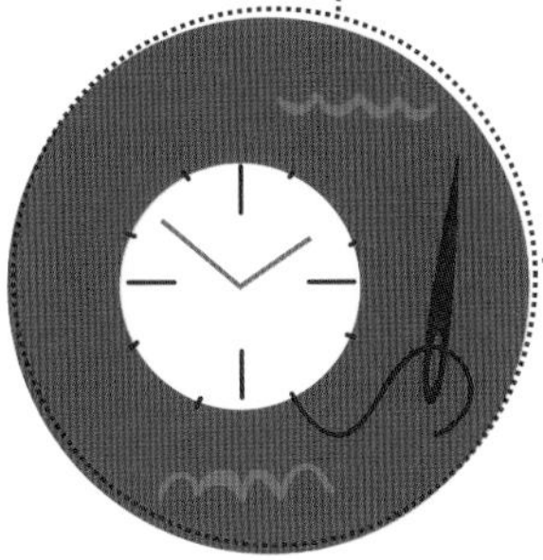

Use a single strand of white floss and tiny overstitches to attach the large control dials to the body invisibly.

NINJABOT

Ninjabot is a pocket-sized crobot warrior. Spare yet elegant in a black matte finish, he carries his staff on his back and his heart—actually his secret weapon—in his hand. His minute headband is held in place by a sparkling sequin and his control panel is a neat red circle on his chest. His expression is bold but endearing—somehow you know that this little fighter will always be on the side of the good guys.

YOU WILL NEED

- crochet hook, size C2 (2.75 mm)
- stitch marker or paper clip
- 1 yarn needle
- 1 embroidery needle
- 1 beading needle
- toy stuffing to stuff the bot
- black yarn
- white yarn
- red yarn
- 1 silver star-shaped sequin
- 1 round silver sequin
- 2 tiny clear beads
- a short wooden stick (this is Ninjabot's traditional staff and can be made from a cut-down Popsicle stick or a tiny length of balsa wood—available at craft stores)
- 2 black bugle beads, ¼ inch (7 mm) long
- black embroidery floss (2 strands)
- red embroidery floss (1 strand)

SKILL LEVEL

TO MAKE NINJABOT

To make the head, using white and black yarn
Face
Start with white yarn
Row 1 ch 10, sc in 2nd ch from hook and in each ch across (9) ch 1 and turn
Rows 2 to 6 sc in each sc across (9) ch 1 and turn
Row 7 sc in each sc across and at the end of the row ch 1 (10)

Work a round of sc on the square, going down left side
sc in next 5 sc, 3 sc in next sc (2nd corner)
sc in next 6 sc, 3 sc in next sc (3rd corner)
sc in next 5 sc (32)

Change to black yarn
Working in blo
sc in next 8 sc and skip one
sc in next 6 sc and skip one
sc in next 8 sc and skip one
sc in next 6 sc and skip one (28)

ABBREVIATIONS: **ch** = *chain* **st** = *stitch* **sl st** = *slip stitch* **sc** = *single crochet* **hdc** = *half-double crochet* **sc dec** = *single crochet decrease (decrease over 2 stitches)* **blo** = *back loops only* ***** = *repeat instructions between asterisks*

Still working in the round, with black yarn
Rounds 1 to 3 sc in each sc around (28)
sl st in next sc and tie off, weave in the end yarn

Back of the head, work with black yarn
As face, repeat up to the end of row 7 (32)
sl st in next sc and tie off, leave long tail to sew to face

To make the body, using red and black yarn
Start with red yarn
Round 1 Start 6 sc in a magic ring (6)
Round 2 2 sc in each sc around (12), sl st in next sc and tie off, weave in the end yarn
Round 3 join black yarn anywhere
2 sc in next sc, sc in next sc repeat 6 times (18)
Round 4 *2 sc in next sc, sc in next 2 sc* repeat 6 times (24)
Rounds 5 to 9 sc in each sc around (24)
Round 10 *sc dec, sc in next 2 sc* repeat 6 times (18)
Round 11 *sc in next sc, sc dec* repeat 6 times (12)
Stuff firmly
Round 12 sc dec around (6)
sl st in next sc and tie off, leave long tail to close up the hole

Make the neck, using black yarn
Round 1 Start 12 sc in a magic ring (12) and tie off
Make two pieces this way and leave long tail for one of them

To make the legs, using black yarn
Round 1 Start 6 sc in a magic ring (6)
Round 2 *2 sc in next sc, sc in next 2 sc* repeat twice (8)
Round 3 in blo sc in each sc around (8)
Rounds 4 to 6 sc in each sc around (8)
Stuff firmly
sl st in next sc and tie off, leave long tail to attach to body
Make 2

To make the arms, using red and black yarn
Start with red yarn
Round 1 Start 4 sc in a magic ring (4)
Round 2 *2 sc in next, sc in next sc* repeat twice (6)
Round 3 sc in each sc around (6)
Round 4 *sc dec, sc in next sc* repeat twice (4)

Change to black yarn
Round 5 *2 sc in next, sc in next sc* repeat twice (6)
Rounds 6 and 7 sc in each sc around (6)
Stuff firmly
sl st in next sc and tie off, leave long tail to attach to body
Make 2

To make the headband, using red yarn
Row 1 ch 28, sc in 2nd ch from hook and in each ch across (27) ch 1 and turn
Row 2 sc in each sc across (27) at the end of each row ch 1 and turn
sl st in next sc and tie off
Leave long tail to join both ends of the headband together

Depending on how tightly you crochet and how firmly you stuff the head, you might want to adjust the length of the headband and crochet more or fewer stitches.

TO ASSEMBLE NINJABOT

- Embroider the face first. Thread the beading needle with two strands of black floss and sew on the two black bugle beads vertically, using the photograph as a guide to place them. Make a short straight stitch at an angle above each eye to make Ninja's eyebrows—they add to his determined look.
- Attach the face to the head using the tail of yarn left over from crocheting. Before closing up, stuff the head firmly, then shape it into a neat rectangular block.
- Sew the two black pieces that compose the neck onto the head with the leftover tail of yarn. Place them precisely in the middle of the head's underside, so that it rests on them in a natural position.

- Attach the body to the neck using a leftover tail of yarn or black floss. Stuff the legs firmly and pin them into place before sewing them onto the body.
- Stuff the arms, pushing the stuffing down to the ends with a toothpick to fill the gloves. Attach the arms to the body, shaping them in a slight curve to make it look as if Ninjabot is ready for action.
- Using one strand of red floss and the beading needle, stitch the silver star-shaped sequin onto Ninjabot's right hand. Thread the sequin onto the needle, follow it with a bead, and stitch back through the center hole of the sequin to secure it in place. Attach the round sequin to his headband in the same way.
- Squeeze Ninjabot's head gently into his headband (it should be a snug fit). Prepare his staff by wrapping a long tail of black yarn a few times around the small wooden stick, then use the end of the yarn to stitch the staff neatly in place on Ninjabot's back.

BLUEPRINT

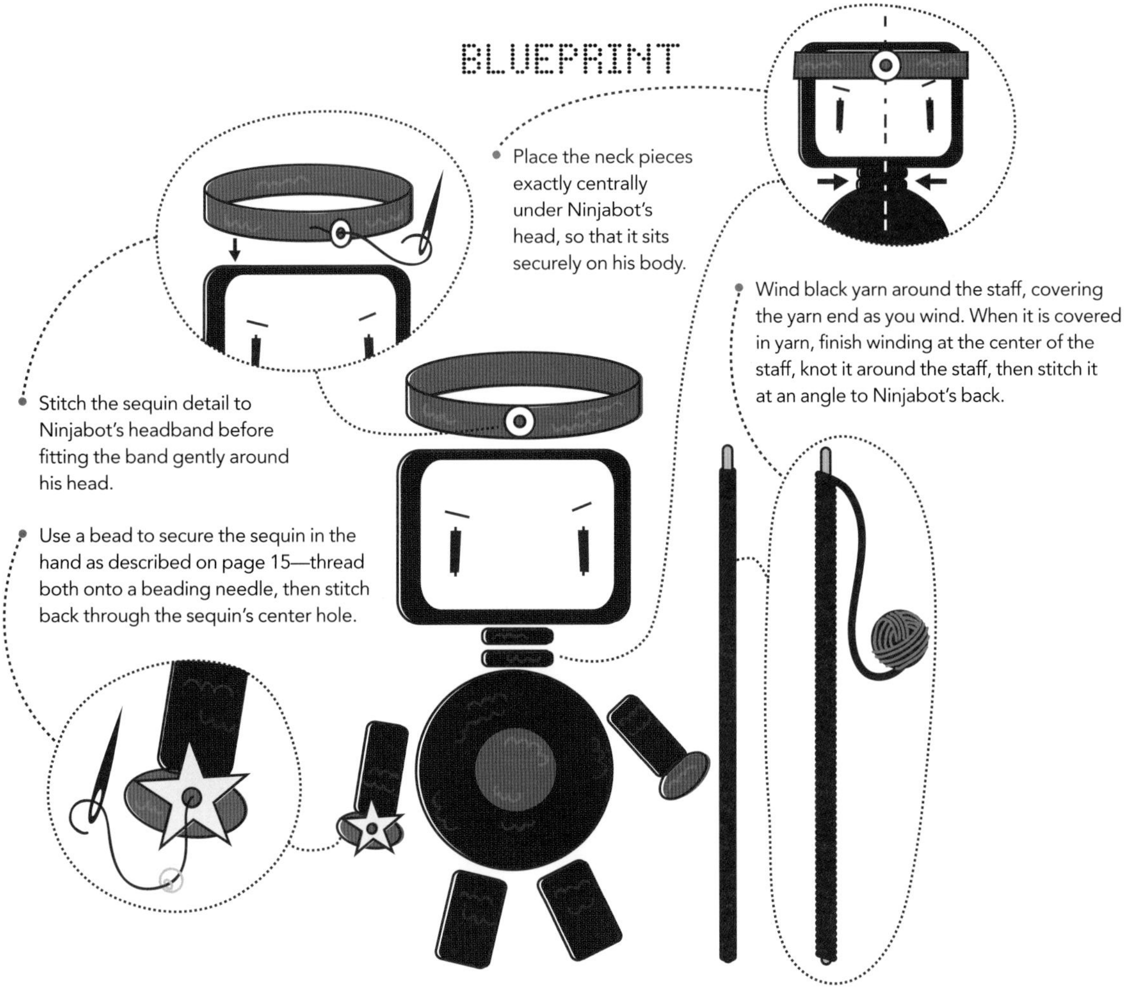
Place the neck pieces exactly centrally under Ninjabot's head, so that it sits securely on his body.
Wind black yarn around the staff, covering the yarn end as you wind. When it is covered in yarn, finish winding at the center of the staff, knot it around the staff, then stitch it at an angle to Ninjabot's back.
Stitch the sequin detail to Ninjabot's headband before fitting the band gently around his head.
Use a bead to secure the sequin in the hand as described on page 15—thread both onto a beading needle, then stitch back through the sequin's center hole.

CATBOT

Catbot has an independent streak, but an affectionate owner can keep her in line with judicious use of her remote control, which is attached to her body with a gleaming metallic cord. She makes a good virtual pet, sitting quietly alongside you, but there's something about her unusual multi-pupil eyes that tells you she's got a mind of her own. If Dogbot is just too docile to suit you, try Catbot for size.

YOU WILL NEED

- crochet hook, size C2 (2.75) mm
- stitch marker or paper clip
- 1 yarn needle
- 1 embroidery needle
- 1 beading needle
- toy stuffing to stuff the bot
- pale blue yarn
- dark blue yarn (for the remote control)
- metallic yarn (for the cord)
- black embroidery floss (2 strands)
- white embroidery floss (1 strand)
- blue embroidery floss (1 strand)
- 3 white beads, ⅛ inch (4 mm) in diameter
- tiny piece of white felt (for the eyes and the front of the remote control)
- 2 tiny red beads
- 6 tiny black beads
- 1 black bugle bead, ¼ inch (7 mm) long
- 2 sequins—1 red, 1 silver

SKILL LEVEL

TO MAKE CATBOT

To make the head, using pale blue yarn
Row 1 ch 12, sc in 2nd ch from hook and in each ch across (11) ch 1 and turn
Rows 2 to 7 sc in each sc across (11) at the end of each row ch 1 and turn
Row 8 sc in next 10 sc, 3 sc in last sc (13)

Now work a round of single crochet on the square, going down left side
sc in next 5 sc, 3 sc in next sc (2nd corner)
sc in next 8 sc, 3 sc in next sc (3rd corner)
sc in next 5 sc, 2 sc in next sc (4th corner) (39)

Now work in the round
Round 9 in blo *sc in each sc around* (39)
Rounds 10 to 12 sc in each sc around (39)
sl st in next sc and tie off, weave in the end yarn

ABBREVIATIONS: **ch** = *chain* **st** = *stitch* **sl st** = *slip stitch* **sc** = *single crochet* **hdc** = *half-double crochet* **sc dec** = *single crochet decrease (decrease over 2 stitches)* **blo** = *back loops only* ***** = *repeat instructions between asterisks*

To make the face, using pale blue yarn
Make the face in the same way as the head, stopping and leaving a long tail of thread at the end of row 8 (you will have 39 sc)

To make the body, using pale blue yarn
Round 1 Start 6 sc in a magic ring (6)
Round 2 2 sc in each sc around (12)
Round 3 *2 sc in next sc, sc in next sc* repeat 6 times (18)
Round 4 in blo *sc dec, sc in next 4 sc* repeat 3 times (15)
Rounds 5 to 8 sc in each sc around (15)
Round 9 *sc dec, sc in next 3 sc* repeat 3 times (12)
Stuff firmly
sl st in next sc and tie off, leave long tail to attach to head

To make the arms and legs, using pale blue yarn
Round 1 Start 4 sc in a magic ring (4)
Round 2 *sc in next sc, 2 sc in next sc* repeat twice (6)
Round 3 sc in each sc around (6)
sl st in next sc and tie off, leave long tail to attach to body
Make 4

To make the ears, using pale blue yarn
Round 1 Start 4 sc in a magic ring (4)
Round 2 2 sc in each sc around (8)
Round 3 *2 sc in next sc, sc in next 3 sc* repeat twice (10)
Round 4 sc in each sc around (10)
No need to stuff, simply flatten the ears
sl st in next sc and tie off, leave long tail to attach to head
Make 2

To make the remote control, using dark blue yarn
Row 1 ch 5, sc in 2nd ch from hook and in each ch across (4) ch 1 and turn
Rows 2 to 15 sc in each sc across (4) ch 1 and turn
sl st in next sc and tie off, leave long tail
Fold in half, stitch sides together, and, before closing up, stuff firmly

To make the cord, using metallic gray yarn
ch 40, leaving a long tail to attach to Catbot's body

TO ASSEMBLE CATBOT

- Cut two tiny squares of white felt for Catbot's eyes. Attach them in position on her face using a single strand of white floss and tiny overstitches.
- Using two strands of black floss and long, straight stitches, embroider Catbot's double pupils, her eyelashes, and her nose.
- When you have completed Catbot's face, sew up the pieces to form her head, using a leftover tail of yarn. Before closing up, stuff firmly, then shape into a neat rectangle. Attach the ears in place, stitching them on with their tails of yarn.
- Stuff the body, then sew the beads and sequins into position using one strand of blue floss. Refer to the photograph to place them neatly. You can either stitch a bead into the center of each sequin or use a contrasting color thread to stitch a star shape with five little stitches into the center of the sequin from the edge.
- Attach Catbot's head to her body using a leftover tail of yarn.
- Stuff the arms and legs and stitch them to the body using their tails of yarn.
- Make the front of the remote control by cutting a tiny piece of white felt to fit. Sew beads on with a single strand of white floss and a beading needle, then use tiny stitches to overlock the felt to the body of the remote control. Stitch the cord onto the remote control and attach the other end in position on Catbot's body.
- Finally attach the cord to the remote and the back of the body.

BLUEPRINT

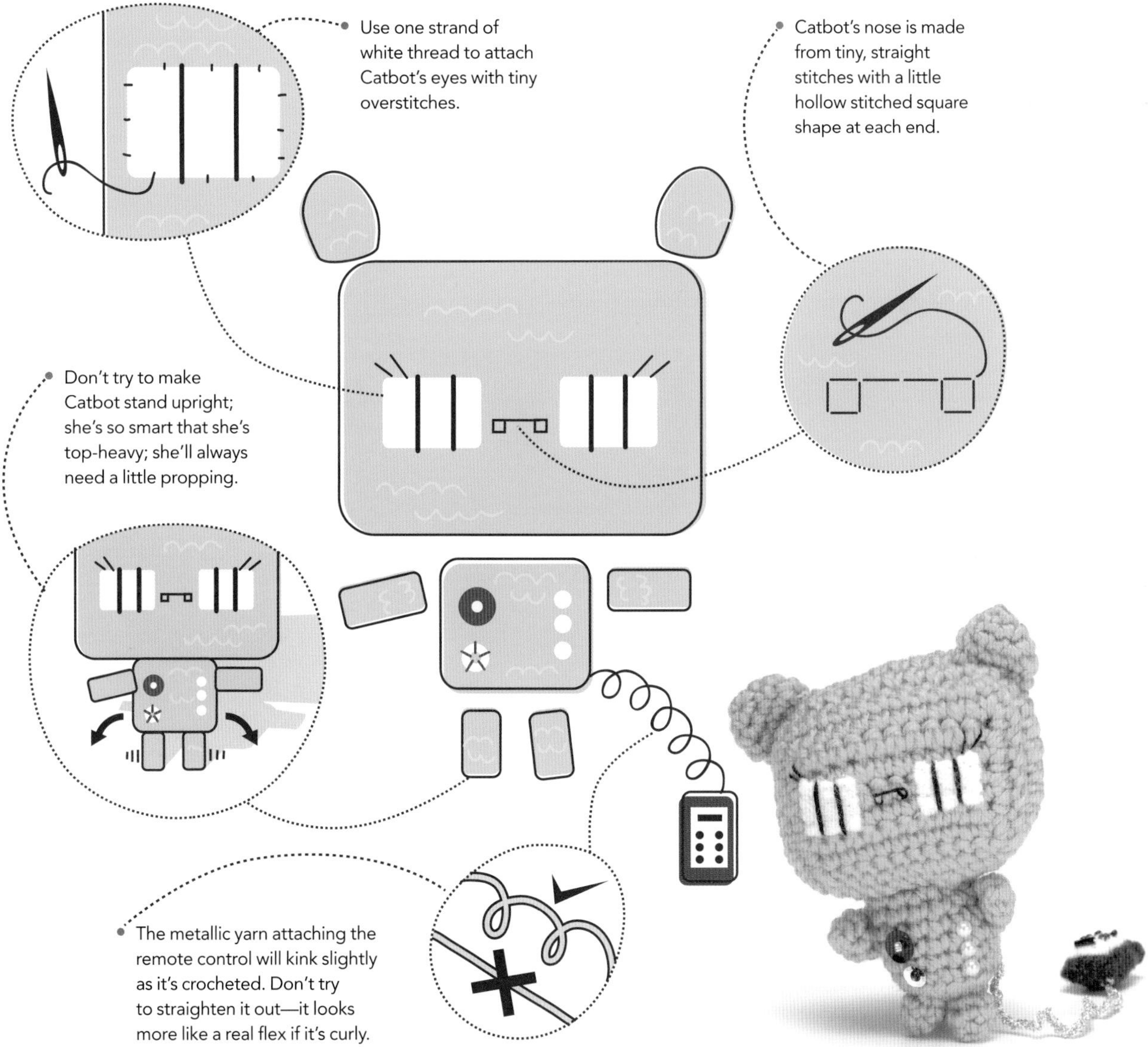
Use one strand of white thread to attach Catbot's eyes with tiny overstitches.
Catbot's nose is made from tiny, straight stitches with a little hollow stitched square shape at each end.
Don't try to make Catbot stand upright; she's so smart that she's top-heavy; she'll always need a little propping.
The metallic yarn attaching the remote control will kink slightly as it's crocheted. Don't try to straighten it out—it looks more like a real flex if it's curly.

GIRLIEBOT

Girliebot is well named—she's as feminine as a sugar-pink color scheme, Lurex detailing, and a handful of glittering sequins can make her. She makes a good companion for Geisha because they share the same impulse to be useful, allied with sweet and ingenuous natures. Consider making both of them and setting them up on a desktop together.

YOU WILL NEED

- crochet hook, size C2 (2.75 mm)
- stitch marker or paper clip
- 1 yarn needle
- 1 embroidery needle
- 1 beading needle
- toy stuffing to stuff the bot
- pink yarn
- purple yarn
- 4 purple buttons, ¾ inch (15 mm) in diameter (for the feet)
- 2 small purple buttons ½ inch (12 mm) in diameter (for the ears)
- black embroidery floss (2 strands)
- red embroidery floss (2 strands)
- metallic purple thread
- 2 black beads, ⅛ inch (4 mm) in diameter
- 2 black sequins
- 4 green sequins
- 1 red sequin
- 4 green beads and one red tiny bead (to secure the sequins in place)
- 2 pins with red bead heads (available at craft stores; use to finish the ears)
- 1 small silver "eye" from a hook-and-eye fastener

SKILL LEVEL

✱✱✱✱

TO MAKE GIRLIEBOT

To make the head, using pink yarn

Round 1 Start 6 sc in a magic ring (6)
Round 2 2 sc in each sc around (12)
Round 3 *2 sc in next sc, sc in next sc* repeat 6 times (18)
Round 4 *2 sc in next sc, sc in next 2 sc* repeat 6 times (24)
Round 5 *2 sc in next sc, sc in next 3 sc* repeat 6 times (30)
Rounds 6 to 9 sc in each sc around (30)
Round 10 *sc dec, sc in next 3 sc* repeat 6 times (24)
Round 11 *sc dec, sc in next 2 sc* repeat 6 times (18)
Round 12 *sc in next sc, sc dec* repeat 6 times (12)
Stuff firmly
Round 13 sc dec around (6)
sl st in next sc and tie off, leave long tail to attach to body

ABBREVIATIONS: **ch** = *chain* **st** = *stitch* **sl st** = *slip stitch* **sc** = *single crochet* **hdc** = *half-double crochet* **sc dec** = *single crochet decrease (decrease over 2 stitches)* **blo** = *back loops only* ***** = *repeat instructions between asterisks*

To make the body, using pink yarn
Round 1 Start 6 sc in a magic ring (6)
Round 2 2 sc in each sc around (12)
Round 3 *2 sc in next sc, 1 sc in next sc* repeat 6 times (18)
Rounds 4 to 8 sc in each sc around (18)
Round 9 *sc in next sc, sc dec* repeat 6 times (12)
Stuff firmly
sl st in next sc and tie off, weave in the end yarn

To make the arms, using purple yarn
Round 1 Start 4 sc in a magic ring (4)
Round 2 *2 sc in next sc, sc in next sc* repeat twice (6)
Round 3 sc in each sc around (6)
sl st in next sc and tie off, leave long tail to sew to body
Make 2 (the arms do not need stuffing)

TO ASSEMBLE GIRLIEBOT

- Stuff the head firmly. Thread an embroidery needle with metallic purple thread and sew two lines around the head: one around the horizontal center, and one around the vertical center. Thread a beading needle with two strands of black floss and sew the eyes in place, first threading on a sequin, then adding a bead and sewing back through the center of the sequin to hold it in place. Using two strands of black floss, embroider the eyelashes and eyebrows. The eyelashes are made with two tiny vertical stitches at a slight angle to the eyes, and the eyebrows are shaped from two short, straight stitches overlapping a little in the middle to create an arch. Use two strands of red floss to make a slightly pouting mouth from a French knot.
- Use pink yarn to sew the small buttons in place on the sides of the head for ears. Press a red-headed pin into the center of each, so it sticks up slightly, like an antenna.
- Stuff the body firmly and secure each sequin with a colored bead as described above. Refer to the picture to place the sequins. Stitch between the sequins with purple metallic thread to complete the control panel. Use pink yarn to attach the silver "eye" to form a little handle to the right of the panel.
- Attach the head and arms to the body using leftover tails of purple yarn.
- Thread a yarn needle with pink yarn, thread two of the larger buttons onto it, and stitch them to the underside of Girliebot to make a leg. Repeat to make the second leg.

BLUEPRINT

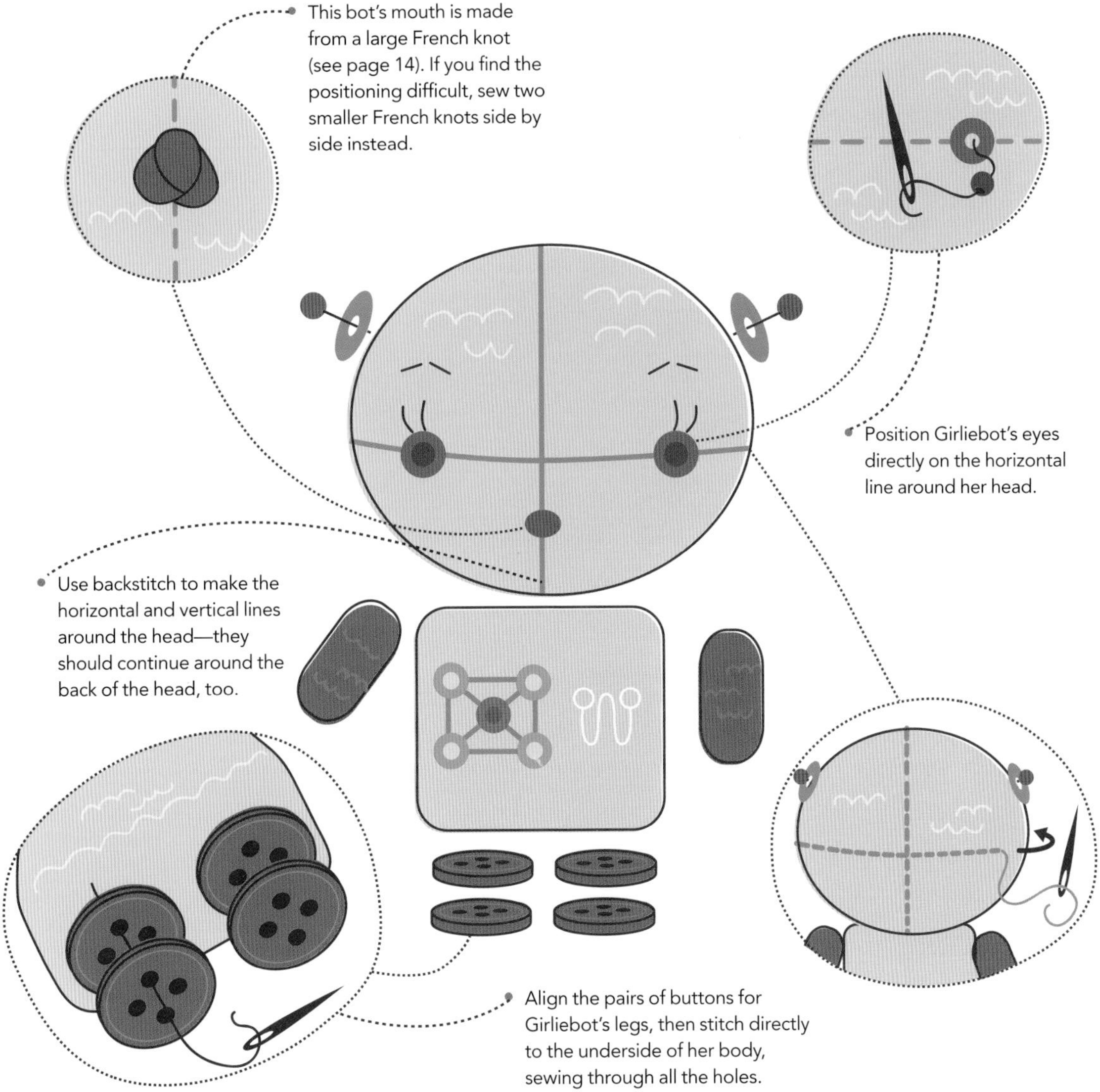

This bot's mouth is made from a large French knot (see page 14). If you find the positioning difficult, sew two smaller French knots side by side instead.

Position Girliebot's eyes directly on the horizontal line around her head.

Use backstitch to make the horizontal and vertical lines around the head—they should continue around the back of the head, too.

Align the pairs of buttons for Girliebot's legs, then stitch directly to the underside of her body, sewing through all the holes.

SUMO

Sumo has a wrestler's build and solid little red legs. His teeny beaded arms are the clearest hint that he's actually a robot (he's one of the few with no obvious control panel). His cheerfully upright crest of hair, sharp black eyes, and waistband all contribute to his name and his status as one of the heavy lifters of the crobot world, ready and able to bear a heavy load.

YOU WILL NEED

- crochet hook, size C2 (2.75 mm)
- stitch marker or paper clip
- 1 yarn needle
- 1 embroidery needle
- 1 beading needle
- green yarn
- red yarn
- black yarn
- gray yarn
- black embroidery floss
- white embroidery floss
- green embroidery floss
- gray embroidery floss
- 2 black beads, ⅛ inch (4 mm) diameter
- 4 green beads, ⅛ inch (4 mm) diameter

SKILL LEVEL

✱✱✱✱

TO MAKE SUMO

To make the head and body, using green yarn

Round 1 Start 6 sc in a magic ring (6)
Round 2 2 sc in each sc around (12)
Round 3 *2 sc in next sc, sc in next 3 sc* repeat 3 times (15)
Rounds 4 to 5 sc in each sc around (15)
Round 6 *2 sc in next sc, sc in next sc* repeat 7 times and finish with 1 sc (22)
Round 7 sc in each sc around (22)
Round 8 *2 sc in next sc, sc in next 10 sc* repeat twice (24)
Rounds 9 to 11 sc in each sc around (24)
Round 12 *2 sc in next sc, sc in next 3 sc* repeat 6 times (30)
Rounds 13 to 15 sc in each sc around (30)
Round 16 *sc dec, sc in next 3 sc* repeat 6 times (24)
Round 17 *sc dec, sc in next 2 sc* repeat 6 times (18)
Round 18 *sc in next sc, sc dec* repeat 6 times (12)
Stuff firmly
Round 19 sc dec around (6)
sl st in next sc and tie off, leave long tail to close up the hole

To make the arms, using red yarn

Round 1 Start 4 sc in a magic ring (4)
Round 2 2 sc in each sc around (8)

ABBREVIATIONS: ch = *chain* **st** = *stitch* **sl st** = *slip stitch* **sc** = *single crochet* **hdc** = *half-double crochet* **sc dec** = *single crochet decrease (decrease over 2 stitches)* **blo** = *back loops only* ***** = *repeat instructions between asterisks*

Round 3 sc dec around (4)
No need to stuff, simply flatten the piece
sl st in next sc and tie off, leave long tail to attach to body
Make 2

To make the legs, using red yarn
Round 1 Start 8 sc in a magic ring (8)
Round 2 2 sc in each sc around (16)
Round 3 sc dec around (8)
Round 4 sc dec around (4)
No need to stuff, simply flatten the pieces
sl st in next sc and tie off
Weave in the end yarn
Make 4

To make the hair, using black yarn
Row 1 ch 10, sc in 2nd ch from hook, then hdc, hdc, dc, dc, dc, hdc, hdc, sc (9)
Tie off, leave long tail to sew to head

To make the topknot, using black yarn
Row 1 ch 10, sc in 2nd ch from hook and in each ch across (9)
Tie off, leave long tail to sew to hair, and fold the piece in half

To make the belt, using gray yarn
Row 1 ch 36, sc in 2nd ch from hook and in each ch across (35)
Tie off, leave long tail to join both ends of the belt together

Second part of the belt
Row 1 ch 20, sc in 2nd ch from hook and in each ch across (19)
Tie off, leave long tail to attach to the middle of the belt

Depending on how tight you crochet and how firmly you stuff the body, you might want to adjust the length of the belt and crochet more or fewer stitches. If you prefer, you can use a piece of ricrac braid or a short length of ribbon.

TO ASSEMBLE SUMO

- First add the facial features. Thread the beading needle with two strands of black floss and sew the two black bead eyes into position on the head, making sure that they are level before stitching. Add small, straight stitches all around each eye to give Sumo his alert, surprised expression.
- Embroider the mouth by threading the sewing needle with two strands of white floss and making a rectangular shape with four or five horizontal straight stitches. Overlap them slightly to get a solid white shape. Thread the needle with two strands of black floss and use backstitch to outline the mouth in black. Then make a few separate vertical straight stitches to show Sumo's teeth.
- Once Sumo has his cheerful, stalwart expression, add his limbs. Thread the sewing needle with one strand of red floss and stitch the two parts of each leg together, then stitch them firmly to the body.
- Sew Sumo's arms to his sides using a leftover tail of yarn. His tiny bead fingers are made from two green beads on each side—thread the beading needle with one strand of green floss and stitch two beads into the center of each arm.
- Add Sumo's hair and topknot. Fold the topknot onto the hairpiece and stitch it into place using a leftover tail of yarn. Position the hair on Sumo's head and stitch it into place.
- Arrange Sumo's belt around his waist and between his legs, then thread a needle with a single strand of gray floss and use a few stitches to fix the belt in place.

BLUEPRINT

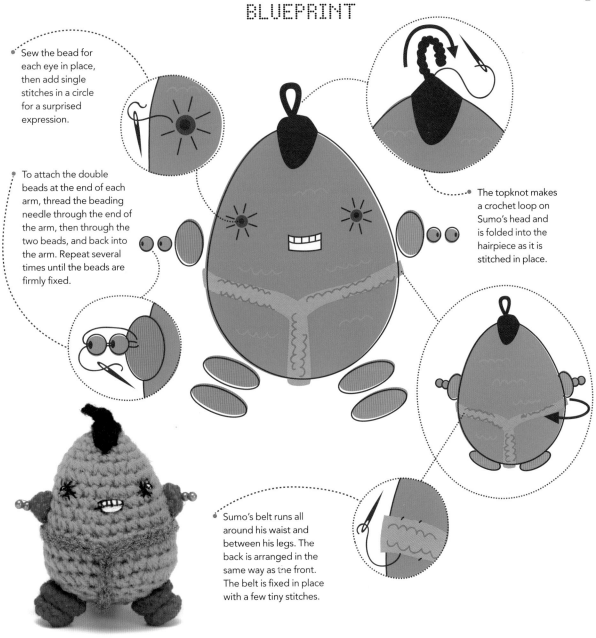

Sew the bead for each eye in place, then add single stitches in a circle for a surprised expression.

To attach the double beads at the end of each arm, thread the beading needle through the end of the arm, then through the two beads, and back into the arm. Repeat several times until the beads are firmly fixed.

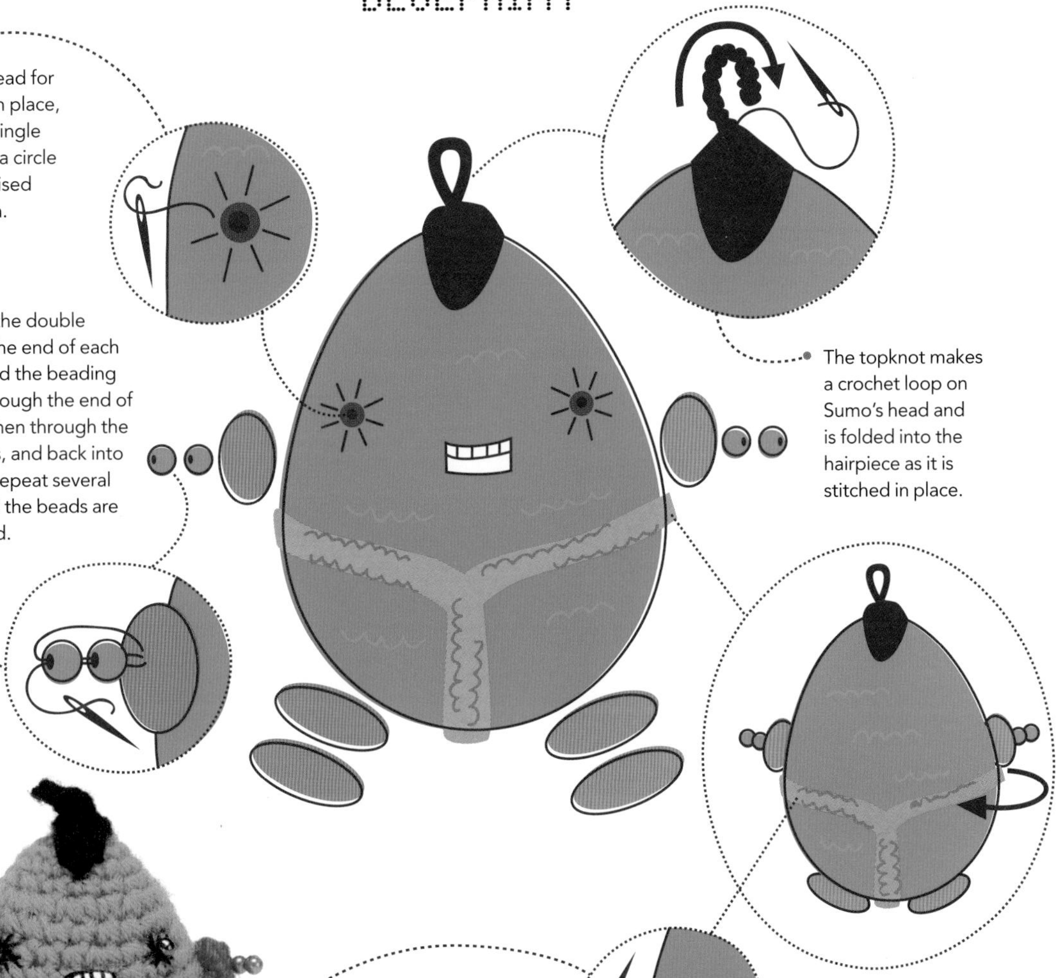

The topknot makes a crochet loop on Sumo's head and is folded into the hairpiece as it is stitched in place.

Sumo's belt runs all around his waist and between his legs. The back is arranged in the same way as the front. The belt is fixed in place with a few tiny stitches.

GEISHA

Sweet, shy, traditional yet robotic, Geisha captures hearts whether she's perching on your desk or taking care of your keys. The fine details give this bot her charm—tiny sandals on her feet, a neat and elaborate hairstyle finished with carefully tied threads, and delicately drawn features. For such a tiny bot, you'll find it easier to assemble the pieces using sewing thread and a small needle, rather than yarn.

YOU WILL NEED

- crochet hook, size C2 (2.75 mm)
- stitch marker or paper clip
- 1 yarn needle
- 1 embroidery needle
- toy stuffing to stuff the bot
- black yarn
- white yarn
- color of your choice for the dress (we chose a subtle eggplant mauve)
- black, white, and red two-strand embroidery floss
- metallic gray embroidery floss
- embroidery floss to match the color of the dress
- sewing thread in black, white, and the same color as the dress

SKILL LEVEL

TO MAKE GEISHA

To make the head, using white yarn
Round 1 Start 6 sc in a magic ring (6)
Round 2 2 sc in each sc around (12)
Round 3 2 sc in each sc around (24)
Round 4 sc in each sc around (24)
Round 5 sc in each sc around (24)
Round 6 *sc in next 5 sc, 2 sc in next sc* repeat 4 times (28)
Round 7 sc in each sc around (28)
Round 8 *sc in next 5 sc, sc dec* repeat 4 times (24)
Round 9 sc dec around (12)
Round 10 sc dec around (6)
sl st in next sc and tie off, weave in the end yarn

To make the hair, using black yarn
Round 1 Start 6 sc in a magic ring (6)
Round 2 2 sc in each sc (12)
Round 3 *2 sc in next sc, sc in next sc* repeat 6 times (18)
Round 4 *2 sc in next sc, sc in next 2 sc* repeat 6 times (24)
Round 5 *sc in next 5 sc, 2 sc in next sc* repeat 4 times (28)
Round 6 sc in each sc around (28)
Round 7 hdc in each sc (28)
Round 8 sc in each hdc (28)
sl st in next sc and tie off, weave in the end yarn

ABBREVIATIONS: ch = *chain* **st** = *stitch* **sl st** = *slip stitch* **sc** = *single crochet* **hdc** = *half-double crochet* **sc dec** = *single crochet decrease (decrease over 2 stitches)* **blo** = *back loops only* * = *repeat instructions between asterisks*

To make the hair buns, using black yarn
Round 1 Start 6 sc in a magic ring (6)
Round 2 2 sc in each sc (12)
Round 3 *2 sc in next sc, 1 sc in next sc* repeat 6 times (18)
Round 4 *sc in next sc, sc dec* repeat 6 times (12)
Round 5 sc dec around (6)
sl st in next sc and tie off, weave in the end yarn
Make 2

To make the body/dress, using the color of your choice
Round 1 Start 6 sc in a magic ring (6)
Round 2 2 sc in each sc around (12)
Round 3 *2 sc in next sc, 1 sc in next sc* repeat 6 times (18)
Round 4 *2 sc in next sc, sc in next 2 sc* repeat 6 times (24)
Round 5 sc in blo just for this round in each sc around (24)
Round 6 sc in each sc around (24)
Round 7 *sc in next 2 sc, sc dec* repeat 6 times (18)
Round 8 *sc in next sc, sc dec* repeat 6 times (12)
Round 9 sc in each sc around (12)
Round 10 sc in each sc around (12)
sl st in next sc and tie off, weave in the end yarn around (12)

To make the arms, using white yarn and the color of the dress
Start with white yarn
Round 1 Start 4 sc in a magic ring (4)
Round 2 *sc in next sc, 2 sc in next sc* repeat twice (6)

Change to the color of the dress
Round 3 sc in each sc around (6)
Round 4 sc in each sc around (6)
Round 5 sc in each sc around (6)
Round 6 sc in each sc around (6)
sl st in next sc and tie off, weave in the end yarn
Make 2

To make the feet, using black yarn
Round 1 Start 4 sc in a magic ring (4)
Round 2 2 sc in each sc around (8)
Round 3 sc in blo for this round in each sc around (8)
Round 4 sc in each sc around (8)
sl st in next sc and tie off, weave in the end yarn
Make 2

TO ASSEMBLE GEISHA

- Getting the happy, tranquil expression of Geisha just right is important, so take care while stitching the face. Start by stuffing the head firmly with scraps of toy stuffing. To help you place the eyes, you can draw them with an air-erasable pen, making sure that they are level on the face.
- Using two strands of black floss, make a single straight stitch for each eye and go over it with a tiny stitch in the middle to give it an arch. Do the same with the eyelashes.
- Still using two strands of black floss, straight stitch the three little hairs of the fringe.
- Thread your needle with two strands of red floss and embroider the mouth, making a diamond shape with four tiny straight stitches. The cheeks are made with French knots.
- Gently squeeze the head into the hair cap. Stuff the buns and sew them onto the sides of the head with the leftover tails of yarn. Using black sewing thread, make a few tiny stitches around the hair cap to secure the hair to the head.
- Stuff the body firmly. Using the metallic gray floss, chain stitch the kimono belt and its diagonal closure. Stuff the head and sew to the body with the remaining tail of yarn.
- Stuff the feet and embroider the shoe details with two strands of white thread, using two straight stitches to make a V shape. Attach feet to body using black sewing thread.
- Stuff the arms and sew them onto the body with sewing thread in the color of the dress.
- Finally, tie threads that match the color of her dress around Geisha's hair buns.

BLUEPRINT

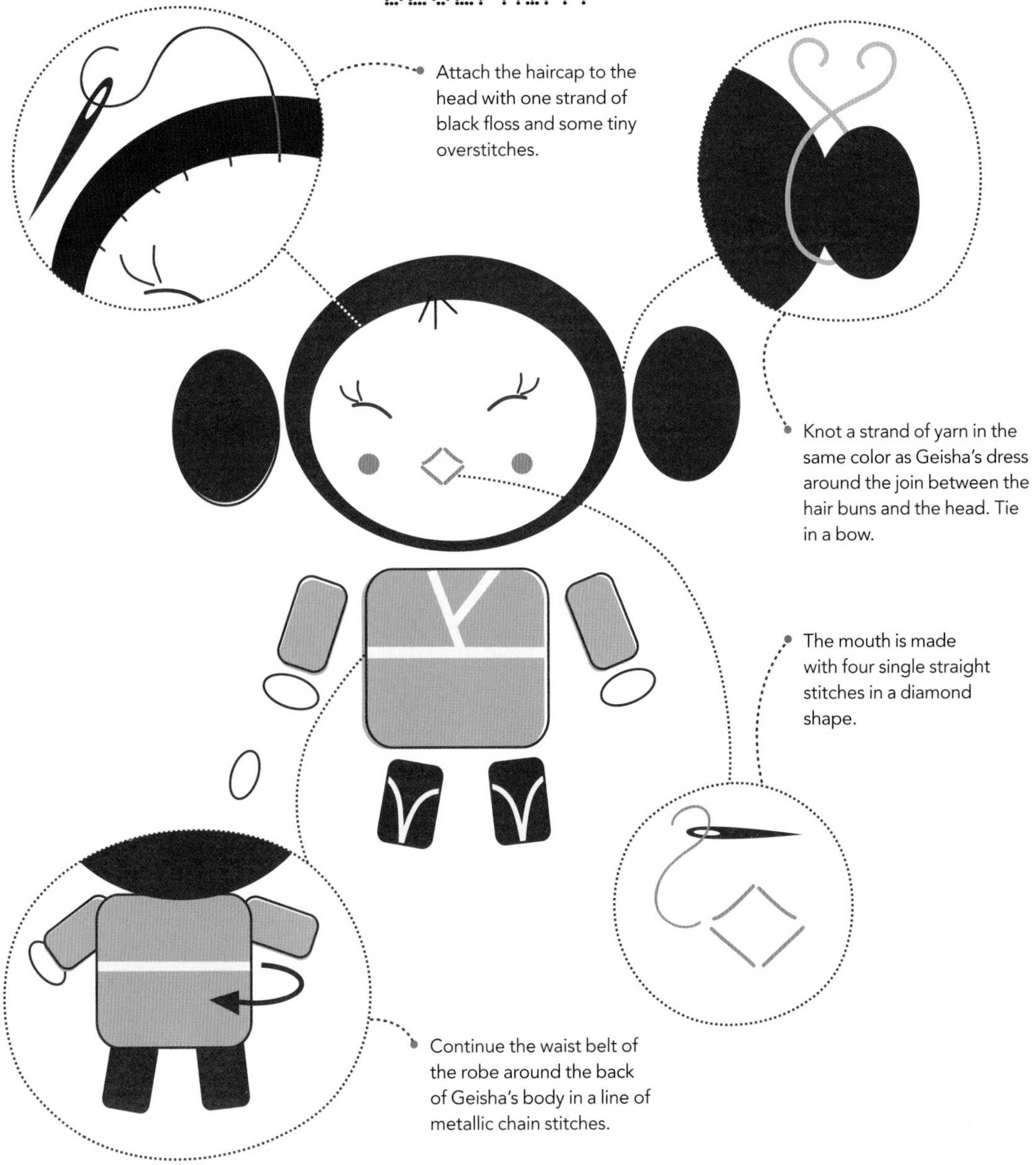
Attach the haircap to the head with one strand of black floss and some tiny overstitches.
Knot a strand of yarn in the same color as Geisha's dress around the join between the hair buns and the head. Tie in a bow.
The mouth is made with four single straight stitches in a diamond shape.
Continue the waist belt of the robe around the back of Geisha's body in a line of metallic chain stitches.

INDEX